A Defense of the Church Institute

A Defense of the Church Institute

Response to the Critics of *Bound to Join*

David J. Engelsma

Reformed Free Publishing Association
Jenison, Michigan

Scriptures cited are taken from the Authorized (King James) Version

Reformed Free Publishing Association
1894 Georgetown Center Drive
Jenison, Michigan 49428–7137
www.rfpa.org
mail@rfpa.org

Book design by Gary Gore Book Design

ISBN 978–1–936054–13–8
LCCN 2012936039

To the Reformed doctrines class,
which has stimulated and encouraged

Contents

Preface

In 2010, the Reformed Free Publishing Association published my book *Bound to Join*.[1] The book demonstrates the importance, indeed, the necessity of membership in an instituted church. The instituted church that believers ought to join is not any church whatever, but a true church. A true church is one that clearly and uncompromisingly shows the marks of a true church of Christ. According to the Reformed creed the Belgic Confession of Faith, these marks are three: "The marks by which the true Church is known are these: If the pure doctrine of the gospel is preached therein; if she maintains the pure administration of the sacraments as instituted by Christ; if church discipline is exercised in punishing of sin."[2]

In the main, the contents of the book were originally a series of letters written to confessing Christians in Europe who, by their own admission, find themselves in unsatisfactory and distressing circumstances regarding church membership. They asked for advice.

The book is practical.

Although there is appeal to a number of passages of Scripture in the book, and even some interpretation of Scripture, the book

1. David J. Engelsma, *Bound to Join: Letters on Church Membership* (Jenison, MI: Reformed Free Publishing Association, 2010).

2. Belgic Confession, Article 29, in Philip Schaff, ed., *Creeds of Christendom with a History and Critical Notes*, 6th ed., 3 vols. (New York: Harper and Row, 1931; repr., Grand Rapids, MI: Baker, 2007), 3:419.

bases its instruction and admonition squarely on Articles 27–29 of the Belgic Confession. The title of the book expresses the book's dependence on the Reformed creed. *Bound to Join* is a phrase in Article 28 of the Belgic Confession: "All men are in duty bound to join and unite themselves with it [the church institute]."[3]

Dependence on the Belgic Confession, as well as other of the Reformed confessions, was deliberate. The Reformed confessions are the authoritative, binding explanation and application of Scripture regarding all doctrines and practices treated by the confessions. All those in Europe to whom the letters were originally sent profess the Reformed religion. The book likewise is mainly directed to Reformed and Presbyterian Christians. The objects of the book's instruction and admonition, therefore, are bound by the Belgic Confession's statements concerning the necessity of church membership.

Objection to the book by persons professing to be Reformed, or Calvinistic, is surprising. Indeed, objection is illegitimate. Articles 27–29 of the Belgic Confession forbid it.

Admittedly, the book is strong medicine. Already when the letters went out to Europe, some reacted angrily against the book's admonition. Especially offensive was my instruction that one must join and remain a member of a true church even at the cost of family relations. But as the proverb has it, desperate illnesses require strong medicine. Living outside and apart from a true church is desperate illness.

Even though the book contains strong medicine, criticism of it by avowed Reformed and Presbyterian Christians is surprising. For the strong medicine is simply the application of the creed: "bound to join."

There has been criticism of the book. Most of it comes from men who are Reformed and Presbyterian. Some of their criticism is sharp, even angry.

---

3. Belgic Confession, Article 28, in ibid., 3:418.

To this criticism, I respond in this little work.

The reason is not at all defense of myself. Self-defense would not warrant the time and energy required by a response or move me to give a response.

But the reason for this response to the criticism is, as the title indicates, defense of the instituted church and of the instruction of the Reformed confession that every one who professes faith in Christ is bound to join a true institute, and never to separate from it.

A defense of the church institute and of membership in it becomes all the more urgent in light of a definite movement, both in Europe and in North America, that boldly rejects the instituted church of Christ and equally boldly denies that anyone needs to be a member of an instituted church. The movement calls itself the "house church" movement. The movement is aggressive and spreading.

When I wrote the book, I was unaware of the breadth and strength of the movement. In light of the house church movement, which is an all-out assault on the beloved bride and precious body of Christ, I am convinced that not only is nothing I wrote in *Bound to Join* too strong, but also that the book might well be stronger in pressing the claim of Christ's church: bound to join.

The Reformed Confessions on the Necessity of Church Membership

"We believe, since this holy congregation is an assemblage of those who are saved, and out of it there is no salvation, that no person of whatsoever state or condition he may be, ought to withdraw himself, to live in a separate state from it; but that all men are in duty bound to join and unite themselves with it; maintaining the unity of the Church; submitting themselves to the doctrine and discipline thereof; bowing their necks under the yoke of Jesus Christ; and as mutual members of the same body, serving to the edification of the brethren, according to the talents God has given them. And that this may be better observed, it is the duty of all believers, according to the Word of God, to separate themselves from those who do not belong to the Church, and to join themselves to this congregation, wheresoever God hath established it, even though the magistrates and edicts of princes be against it; yea, though they should suffer death or bodily punishment" (Belgic Confession, Article 28).

"The visible Church, which is also catholic or universal under the gospel (not confined to one nation as before under the law) consists of all those, throughout the world, that profess the true religion, and of their children; and is the kingdom of the Lord Jesus Christ, the house and family of God, out of which there is no ordinary possibility of salvation" (Westminster Confession of Faith, Chapter 25.2).

"*Outside the Church of God There Is No Salvation.* But we esteem fellowship with the true Church of Christ [the marks of which are given in the preceding paragraph, 'especially the lawful and sincere preaching of the Word of God'] so highly that we deny that those can live before God who do not stand in fellowship with the true Church of God, but separate themselves from it. For as there was no salvation outside Noah's ark when the world perished in the flood; so we believe that there is no certain salvation outside Christ, who offers himself to be enjoyed by the elect in the Church; and hence we teach that those who wish to live ought not to be separated from the true Church of Christ" (Second Helvetic Confession, Chapter 17).

"*What Ought to Be Done in Meetings for Worship.* Although it is permitted all men to read the Holy Scriptures privately at home, and by instruction to edify one another in the true religion, yet in order that the Word of God may be properly preached to the people, and prayers and supplication publicly made, also that the sacraments may be rightly administered, and that collections may be made for the poor and to pay the cost of all the Church's expenses, and in order to maintain social intercourse, it is most necessary that religious or Church gatherings be held. For it is certain that in the apostolic and primitive Church, there were such assemblies frequented by all the godly.

"*Meetings for Worship Not to Be Neglected.* As many as spurn such meetings and stay away from them, despise true religion, and are to be urged by the pastors and godly magistrates to abstain from stubbornly absenting themselves from sacred assemblies" (Second Helvetic Confession, Chapter 22).

"That thou mayest know how thou oughtest to behave thyself in the house of God, which is the church of the living God, the pillar and ground of the truth."

—1 Timothy 3:15

A Defense of the Church Institute

CHAPTER ONE

_◡♈◞_

Criticism by Those at Ease
outside of Zion

THE FIRST CRITICISM of _Bound to Join_ is simply angry denunciation of the book and its author by some who live outside the church and who refuse to move to an area where
they could be members of a true church, because moving would be
painful and costly.

These critics either are members of no church whatever or, by
their own admission, are members of, or attend, churches that lack
the marks of the true church. In some cases the churches they attend
are charismatic, Arminian, and Baptist. These are the only churches
that are available to the critics where they live.

For some of these critics, both in Europe and in North America,
moving to an area where membership in a true church is possible
would not require leaving the country for a foreign land, but only
moving some distance across their own country. This would involve
some hardship, to be sure, but not extreme hardship.

These critics are strong Calvinists, doctrinally, or so they say. They
are fierce foes of Arminianism and Romanism. They are well-read. In
their hearts, they say, they worship God according to the Reformed
religion.

If a true church were nearby, so that membership would be convenient, no doubt they would join. Since this is not the case, they are
content to live and die outside the church.

They do not need the church. They express a _desire_ for the church.
But they do not _need_ the church.

Against the admonition of *Bound to Join* that church membership is necessary, these persons react with indignation.

They appeal to their membership in the universal, invisible church of Jesus Christ, the company of the elect, which the Son of God gathers out of the nations throughout history.

Their chief argument against the book, however, is purely personal and emotional: "The book judges me to be unsaved, even though I profess to be a believer and am, in fact, an ardent Calvinist, doctrinally. The book is harsh. The author is hardhearted."

My response to these critics is that I press the charge and urge them to take it with utmost seriousness: "Outside the instituted, true church of Jesus Christ, there is no salvation!" I want them and all others who are in their situation regarding church membership to hear this charge, so that they repent of their sin against the church and her head. Then in true repentance they will also do whatever is necessary, whatever the cost, to become members of the church.

I remind them that the judgment "outside the church is no salvation" is not mine, as though I came up with it. It is the official, authoritative judgment of the Reformed faith. The Belgic Confession of Faith, drawn up in 1561 and adopted by the ecumenical Synod of Dordt in 1618–19, declares: "Out of it [that is, out of the true institute] there is no salvation." The Reformed creed immediately adds the practical admonition: "All men are in duty bound to join and unite themselves with it."[1]

The Church Universal

The appeal of these critics to their membership in the invisible, universal body of Christ is mistaken. The mistake is not their confession that the church is the universal body of Christ, made up of all those whom God has elected in Christ in eternity. Nor is their mis-

1. Belgic Confession, Article 28, in ibid., 3:418.

take that they describe the universal body and bride of Christ as presently invisible. It certainly is not their mistake that they suppose that it is important to know oneself as a member of this universal body.

But their mistake is that they claim membership in this universal body *while despising and rejecting the institutional form of this universal body.*

The church of Jesus Christ is the total number of the elect as eternally known and chosen by God to be the well-formed bride and perfectly formed body of her husband and head, Jesus Christ. This is what the church is *essentially.* The martyr John Hus and the reformers referred to the church as "the company of the predestinated." The first article charged against Hus by the papal church at the Council of Constance in 1415 and for which teaching they burned him was Hus' doctrine: "The catholic or universal church is [composed] of the predestinate only."[2]

Against the false doctrine of the church of Rome that the church is exclusively a visible organization—the *Roman Catholic* organization—the Reformed faith confesses that the church is the body of the elect, which the Son of God gathers unto himself by his word and Spirit from the beginning to the end of the world. This universal, or catholic, church is invisible to us. We will see it for the first time in the day of Christ, when the great multitude that no man can number, out of all nations, stands before the throne of God and before the Lamb (Rev. 7:9).

With the truth that the church is the universal body of the elect, John Calvin begins his treatment of the doctrine of the church in book 4 of the *Institutes.* "The article in the Creed in which we profess to 'believe the church' refers not only to the visible church (our

---

2. Quoted in Matthew Spinka, *John Hus' Concept of the Church* (Princeton, NJ: Princeton University Press, 1966), 347. In Hus' own words, his teaching was: "The holy catholic, i.e., universal Church, is the totality of the predestinate" (Spinka, *John Hus,* 347).

present topic) but also to all God's elect, in whose number are also included the dead."[3]

That this universal church of the elect is invisible, according to Calvin, is clearly implied by the contrast between it and the "visible church": "The article in the Creed...refers not only to the *visible* church" (emphasis added). Calvin expresses that the universal church is invisible when he describes the unity of this church.

> To embrace the unity of the church in this way, we need not (as we have said) see the church with the eyes or touch it with the hands. Rather, the fact that it belongs to the realm of faith should warn us to regard it no less since it passes our understanding *than if it were clearly visible.* And our faith is no worse because it recognizes a church beyond our ken.[4]

The Heidelberg Catechism confesses the church as the universal body of the elect gathered by Christ throughout history:

> What dost thou believe concerning the Holy Catholic Church?
>
>   That out of the whole human race, from the beginning to the end of the world, the Son of God, by his Spirit and Word, gathers, defends, and preserves for himself unto everlasting life, a chosen communion in the unity of the true faith; and that I am, and forever shall remain, a living member of the same.[5]

3. John Calvin, *Institutes of the Christian Religion*, ed. John T. McNeill, trans. Ford Lewis Battles (Philadelphia: Westminster Press, 1960), 4.1.2, 2:1012–13.

4. Ibid., 4.1.3, 2:1015; emphasis added.

5. Heidelberg Catechism, Q&A 54, in Schaff, *Creeds of Christendom*, 3:324–25.

Likewise, the Belgic Confession takes up the doctrine of the church by affirming that the church is universal; that her membership is "true Christian believers"; and that the unity of the church, as the union of her members, is spiritual and, therefore, invisible.

> We believe and profess one catholic or universal Church, which is a holy congregation and assembly of true Christian believers, expecting all their salvation in Jesus Christ, being washed by his blood, sanctified and sealed by the Holy Ghost. This Church hath been from the beginning of the world, and will be to the end thereof...Furthermore, this holy Church is not confined, bound, or limited to a certain place or to certain persons, but is spread and dispersed over the whole world; and yet is joined and united with heart and will, by the power of faith, in one and the same spirit.[6]

In confessing the church as the body of all the elect, the Reformed creeds are expressing the teaching of the Bible in such a passage as Ephesians 5:25, 27: "Christ also loved the church, and gave himself for it...That he might present it to himself a glorious church, not having spot, or wrinkle, or any such thing; but that it should be holy and without blemish." In light of Ephesians 1:4, the members of the church whom Christ loved and for whom he gave himself are all those, and those only, whom God elected in Christ as the body and bride of Christ in eternity: "He [God] hath chosen us in him [Christ] before the foundation of the world, that we should be holy and without blame before him."

The error of the critics of *Bound to Join* who are now in view, therefore, is not their estimation of the universal church.

---

6. Belgic Confession, Article 27, in ibid., 3:416–17.

The Church Institute

But the critics ignore that the universal body of Christ takes visible, organizational form in history as the instituted congregation. The instituted congregation is an assembly of believers and their children that is established in, governs itself by, and functions through three special offices—pastor, elder, and deacon—and that meets for the public worship of God on the Lord's day. Public worship is the main calling of the congregation. Basic to this public worship are the preaching and hearing of the pure doctrine of the gospel and the administration and use of the sacraments.

The church of the decree of election must be gathered, out of the ungodly world and out of the natural state of guilt and natural condition of total depravity of the members of the church, into the communion of her husband and head, Jesus Christ. When Christ gathers the church of the elect, he not only brings the individual elect to faith and salvation, but he also forms congregations, in which the believer and his family are preserved in salvation and edified and with which the individual believer can carry out the high calling of the public worship of God.

Acts 14:23 teaches that the nature of apostolic missions was the instituting of churches by the ordaining of elders: "And when they had ordained them elders in every church…" Philippians 1:1 teaches not only that the gathering of the church by Christ proceeds by the institution of congregations with bishops and deacons, but also that all the saints are expected to be members of instituted congregations: "Paul and Timotheus…to all the saints in Christ Jesus which are at Philippi, with the bishops and deacons."

Indeed, Christ performs the work of gathering the elect church *by means of the instituted congregation*. Such is the worth of the church institute, which these critics despise and reject or, in the case of some, ignore. According to Romans 10:13–17, Christ gathers the elect church by means of the office of the preaching of the gospel:

"How then shall they call on him in whom they have not believed? and how shall they believe in him…whom they have not heard? and how shall they hear without a preacher? And how shall they preach except they be sent?"

But the office of preaching inheres in and belongs to the instituted congregation. According to the Belgic Confession, the office of preaching, with that of the ruling elder and that of the deacon, fixed in the church institute, is nothing less than the "spiritual policy which our Lord has taught us in his Word."

> We believe that this true Church must be governed by the spiritual policy which our Lord has taught us in his Word—namely, that there must be Ministers or Pastors to preach the Word of God, and to administer the Sacraments; also elders and deacons, who, together with the pastors, form the council of the Church; that by these means the true religion may be preserved, and the true doctrine every where propagated, likewise transgressors punished and restrained by spiritual means; also that the poor and distressed may be relieved and comforted, according to their necessities.[7]

Implied by this article of the Reformed confession is that one who despises and rejects the institute despises and rejects "the spiritual policy" of Christ, by which Christ purposes to govern all his people.

That the church is the body of the elect is the truth about the church, but it is not the full truth. The full truth is that the church is the body of the elect, *which manifests itself as, or takes form in, the instituted congregation.* Such is the relation of the elect body and the local congregation, instituted in the three special offices, that the

7. Belgic Confession, Article 30, in ibid., 3:421–22.

congregation *is* the universal body of the elect *as this universal body takes form in the world.* The local congregation is the visible form of the invisible company of the predestinated.

One Church

This is the implication of the oneness of the church. The oneness of the church is a fundamental perfection of the church according to Scripture: "one body" (Eph. 4:4). The Spirit of Christ led the early Christian church to confess the oneness of the church from her earliest post-apostolic days. "I believe…the [one] holy catholic Church."[8] "And [I believe] one Holy Catholic and Apostolic Church."[9]

In Scripture both the universal body composed of all the elect and the instituted congregation are called "the church." When Jesus declared that he would build "my church" on the rock of Peter's confession that Jesus is "the Christ, the Son of the living God" (Matt. 16:16, 18) and when the apostle wrote that "Christ also loved the church, and gave himself for it" (Eph. 5:25), the reference was not to any institution, but to the universal body and bride of the decree of election. The company of the predestinated, which is gathered by Christ throughout history out of all nations as true believers and the elect, regenerated children of believers, is "the church."

But so also is every true institute "the church." The local, instituted congregation in Corinth was "the church of God which is at Corinth" (1 Cor. 1:2). To that institute, the apostle announced, "Now ye are the body of Christ" (1 Cor. 12:27). This is extraordinarily significant, even seemingly daring, language. To a local congregation, and then a local congregation troubled by schisms and gross iniquity, the apostle applies the glorious description, indeed

8. The Apostles' Creed, in ibid., 2:45.
9. The Nicaeno-Constantinopolitan Creed, in ibid., 2:59.

definition, that belongs in the first instance to the church as she appears in the decree of election: "body of Christ"!

The apostle did not say, "Ye are part of the body," which itself would have been an honorific description. But he said, "Ye, the institute at Corinth, *are the body of Christ*." No one who slights, neglects, or ignores the instituted church believes these words. Much less do those who despise and reject the institute.

In his second epistle to the Corinthians, the apostle applies to the congregation at Corinth the other outstanding description of the universal church of Christ: bride. That the universal church of the elect is the bride of Christ is the teaching of Ephesians 5:22–33, where the apostle makes marriage the symbol of the covenant relation of love between Christ and the church: "Husbands, love your wives, even as Christ also loved the church…I speak concerning Christ and the church" (vv. 25, 32). In 2 Corinthians 11:1–4, the apostle describes the Corinthian congregation as the bride, or wife, of Christ. "I have espoused you to one husband, that I may present you as a chaste virgin to Christ" (v. 2).

The explanation of Scripture's calling both the universal body of the elect and the local congregation "the church" cannot be that they are two distinct churches. For the church is one. But the explanation is that the local congregation is the one church of Christ *as a manifestation, a visible form,* of the universal body of the elect, which is being gathered by the Son of God.

It is this oneness of the instituted congregation with the universal body of Christ that explains the otherwise inexplicable and even objectionable movement of the Belgic Confession from universal body of Christ, which is invisible, to visible institute in Articles 27 and 28. At the end of Article 27, the Belgic Confession is plainly referring to the universal body of Christ as she is gathered by the Son of God throughout history and over all the world. The church of Article 27 consists only of believers who are washed by Jesus' blood and sealed by the Holy Ghost. It is the church that is "spread and dispersed over the whole world."

The church in view already at the very beginning of Article 28 is the local, instituted congregation, for it is the congregation that one can "withdraw" from "to live in a separate state from" it, and the congregation that one is "duty bound to join." It is the congregation with "doctrine and discipline." In this congregation members serve other members with their gifts. It is the congregation that "God hath established." Such is the visibility of this congregation that wicked magistrates take note of it, so as to persecute it.

These things are true only of the institute. One cannot withdraw from the church of election. Nor does he join the body of the elect. It is the institute to which Christ gives doctrine and discipline. Members of the local congregation function with their talents and gifts on behalf of the other members and, thus, on behalf of the entire congregation.

Theologians have criticized the Belgic Confession for what they consider an abrupt and puzzling move from the catholic church of Article 27 to the instituted church of Article 28. Some have even proposed a revision of these articles.

But wrongly!

The Confession is simply expressing the biblical doctrine of the church. The catholic body of the elect *takes form* in the local congregation. The institute *is* the catholic body in its manifestation of itself in the world. The same "difficulty" of distinguishing the universal body of believers and the local congregation that is alleged against the Belgic Confession as a fault is inherent in Scripture.

To what does the apostle refer in Ephesians 4:1–5 when he exhorts the Ephesian believers and their children to endeavor "to keep the unity of the Spirit in the bond of peace," appealing to the "one body"? Certainly, he refers to the unity of the local congregation in Ephesus, which was the "one body" of Christ in that city. And this is a sharp rebuke of those who neglect, or reject, the institute. They do nothing on behalf of the unity of the Spirit. They certainly do not exert themselves on behalf of unity, as is the meaning of "endeavouring" in Ephesians 4:3.

But who will contend that the unity of the Spirit on behalf of the one body in Ephesians 4:3–4 has nothing to do with the universal church of elect believers that Christ was gathering throughout the Mediterranean world at that time and that he is gathering everywhere in the world today? Ultimately, the reference is to this universal church. The language itself suggests this: "unity of the Spirit," which is not limited to the church at Ephesus in the first century AD; "one body," which the Ephesian congregation manifested but did not exhaust.

That the reference is ultimately to the universal church being gathered by Christ is put beyond doubt by verse 13, which shows that the apostle has in view nothing less than the "perfect man." The perfect man is the new humanity in Jesus Christ of the elect out of all nations, who come at last to the "measure of the stature of the fulness of Christ."

Such is the relation of the institute and the universal body of Christ—*the oneness of the church*—that the believer who endeavors to keep the unity of the Spirit in the congregation is, by this fact, keeping the unity of the Spirit in the universal, invisible church of elect believers and their children throughout the world. *By* his or her meek conduct in the congregation, as well as by all the other behavior that makes for unity, he or she promotes the unity of the catholic body of Christ in the world.

Now all of this truth about the relation of the universal body of the elect and the institute must be applied to the critics of *Bound to Join* who neglect, and even reject, the local congregation.

Christ gathers the universal church of election by forming congregations and by placing elect individuals who have been brought to faith in a local congregation. One way he places elect, believing members in a local congregation is by confronting them with the urgent calling of Article 28 of the Belgic Confession: "bound to join." So insistent is Christ that every one of his own belong to his church, the local congregation, and so aware of the sluggishness of some and of the difficulties of others, that he adds the solemn warning of Article 28: "Out of it [the local congregation] there is no salvation."

If one is and knows himself to be a member of the universal body of Christ, he will love that church *in her institutional form*. The church is one. To confess love for the church of the decree of election but to neglect and ignore, or even to despise and reject, her institutional form is as though a man would profess love for the *idea* of his wife but ignore and neglect, or even despise and reject, her bodily form—by deliberately living apart from her. The rejection of the bodily reality of the wife gives the lie to his profession of love for the idea of her. It is also consummate folly. What husband does not want the bodily form of his wife, does not want to live with her, indeed, will not do anything short of denying Christ to live with her?

Assurance in the Institute

Outside the church institute one cannot have assurance that he is a member of the universal church. The elect believer certainly can have, ought to have, and does have assurance of belonging to the universal body of the elect. He knows not only that he is a member in good standing of a local congregation, but also that he is a living member of the body and bride of Jesus Christ that God chose unto eternal life. In question and answer 54 of the Heidelberg Catechism, every believing child of God confesses the certainty of faith concerning his own membership not in some local congregation or other, but in the company of the elect that Christ is gathering by his Spirit and word: "and that I am, and forever shall remain, a living member of the same [the 'chosen communion']."[10]

What must not be overlooked and ignored is that the believer

10. Heidelberg Catechism, Q&A 54, in ibid., 3:324–25.

who thus expresses his assurance of membership in the universal body of Christ *is a baptized member of a true institute.* As a member of an instituted church, he has the kingdom of heaven opened to him Sunday after Sunday by the preaching of the gospel. "What is the Office of the Keys? The preaching of the holy Gospel and Church discipline; by which two things the kingdom of heaven is opened to believers and shut against unbelievers."[11] One who is not a member of an instituted church, of course, lacks the regular preaching of the gospel, to say nothing of "church discipline," and thus the opening up of the kingdom to him.

As a member of an instituted church, by the weekly preaching of the gospel the believer is blessed with the maintenance and strengthening of his faith, including his faith that he is a member of the universal body of the elect. "Since, then, we are made partakers of Christ and all his benefits by faith only, whence comes this faith? The Holy Ghost works it in our hearts by the preaching of the holy Gospel, and confirms it by the use of the holy Sacraments."[12]

If he is an adult member of the institute, the one who confesses faith concerning his membership in the universal body of the elect in question and answer 54 of the Catechism is the man who has his faith confirmed, or strengthened, by his obedient use of the sacrament of the Lord's supper. This is the teaching of the Heidelberg Catechism in the question and answer just quoted: "and confirms it [faith] by the use of the holy Sacraments."

The regular confirmation of the faith of the believer by the sacrament of the supper is a strengthening of his faith not only that he is justified and sanctified, but also that he is a member of the elect body of Christ.

> What is it to eat the crucified body and drink the shed blood of Christ?

---

11. Heidelberg Catechism, Q&A 83, in ibid., 3:337.
12. Heidelberg Catechism, Q&A 65, in ibid., 3:328.

It is not only to embrace with a believing heart all the
sufferings and death of Christ, and thereby to obtain the
forgiveness of sins and life eternal, *but moreover, also, to be
so united more and more to his sacred body by the Holy Ghost,
who dwells both in Christ and in us, that although he is in
heaven, and we on the earth, we are nevertheless flesh of his
flesh and bone of his bones, and live and are governed forever
by one Spirit, as members of the same body are by one soul.*[13]

One who neglects or refuses to be a member of an instituted
church not only is disobedient to the command of the Lord Jesus
to partake of the sacrament, "Take, eat…Drink ye all of it" (Matt.
26:26–27), and thus "shew the Lord's death till he come" (1 Cor.
11:26). He also deprives himself of the confirmation of faith concerning membership in the elect body of Christ.

The assurance of membership in the universal body of the elect
arises out of the bosom of the church institute. Outside the church
institute, no one can confidently say, "I am, and forever shall remain,
a living member of the [chosen communion of Christ]."

Salvation in the Institute

But Article 28 of the Belgic Confession teaches not only that
there is no *assurance* of salvation outside the instituted church (which
is grievous enough). The Reformed creed, faithfully expressing the
teaching of the Bible, as all Reformed Christians acknowledge, also
teaches that there is no *salvation* outside the instituted church.

No more than physical life is spiritual life a matter of a once-
for-all-time act of God. Like God's gift of physical life, the gift of
salvation is ongoing and lifelong. Just as God sustains physical life,

13. Heidelberg Catechism, Q&A 76, in ibid., 3:332; emphasis added.

heals it when it becomes sick, and works marvelous growth and development, so also does he save. Having regenerated his elect child, God nourishes, sustains, develops, and matures the spiritual life of the regenerated child. This too is *salvation*. When Paul proclaims in Ephesians 2:8 "by grace are ye saved," his meaning is that the elect have been saved in the past and continue to be saved in the present by grace.

For the maintaining and increase of our physical life, God uses means. We know what these means are and use them diligently. No one, even in earliest childhood, says, "I am alive and therefore I refuse to eat and drink; I even refuse any longer to breathe in God's air." When he is seriously sick, no adult in his right mind refuses to seek treatment from a competent doctor because, after all, "I am alive; I received the gift of life from God once upon a time." The man or woman who chooses to live outside a home in the wind and weather is rightly regarded as mentally ill and usually dies young.

It is no different with regard to spiritual life (I leave out of consideration the exception, for example, the elect infant in the womb who dies immediately upon being born again by God). God saves his people continuously from the moment of the new birth to the moment of victory over death and passage into glory. (And then he keeps saving us to all eternity.) For his saving work in this life, God uses means. These means are the preaching of the gospel, the administration of the sacraments, and in certain circumstances of extreme spiritual sickness the discipline of the elders.

These means are given by God to, and exercised by, the instituted church!

Believing children of God can and do use and benefit from these means *only in the instituted church*!

God saves his people continuously *as members of the church institute, by diligent use of the means of grace*!

This is the explanation of the strong, but really unsurprising, statement by the Belgic Confession, echoed by *Bound to Join*, that outside the church institute is no salvation.

This is the truth that the critics of *Bound to Join* resist.

I will not prove from Scripture that God uses the means of preaching and sacraments, which, of course, are found in the church institute, to save his people. I easily could do so.

I could point to the obvious fact that all the New Testament— from the history of missions in Acts, through the various epistles *addressed to instituted congregations*, to the book of Revelation, which begins with letters to seven instituted churches with officebearers— teaches that believers and their children are and are expected to be members of an instituted church, in which they are saved by the word of God and the sacraments.

I could quote Romans 10:13–17 in support of the truth that faith comes by hearing the word of God and that this word of God is the preaching of the gospel by a man called by Christ through the church institute. Rightly translated, in verse 14 this passage explains the reason believers must always be hearing the preaching: the preaching of the gospel by an ordained man is the living voice of Christ himself.

I could appeal to the great church epistle—Ephesians—to demonstrate, conclusively, that the ascended Christ now gives "pastors and teachers," that is, pastors who teach "for the perfecting of the saints, for the work of the ministry, for the edifying of the body of Christ: Till we all come in the unity of the faith, and of the knowledge of the Son of God, unto a perfect man, unto the measure of the stature of the fulness of Christ" (Eph. 4:11–13).

I could adduce the pastoral epistles at length in proof of the contention of *Bound to Join*, which is challenged by its critics, that God saves his people within the instituted church by the labor of pastors and elders. I could direct the attention of the critics of *Bound to Join* to 1 Timothy 4:16, where the apostle states *explicitly* that pastor Timothy "saves" himself and the members of his congregation by his doctrine. I could refer the critics to 1 Timothy 5:17 and to Titus

1:5, where the necessity of the teaching and oversight of elders for salvation is indicated. I could urge the critics to consider 1 Timothy 3:15, which is so far from sharing their low estimation of the local congregation that the text calls the instituted congregation "the house of God...the church of the living God, the pillar and ground of the truth."

But I do not. Rather, I confront the critics with the official, authoritative, binding testimony about the instituted church and the means of grace and salvation of the Reformed confessions. Most, if not all, of the critics claim to be Calvinistic—Reformed or Presbyterian. All, therefore, are bound by the creeds.

Since, then, we are made partakers of Christ and all his benefits by faith only, whence comes this faith?

The Holy Ghost works it in our hearts by the preaching of the holy Gospel, and confirms it by the use of the holy Sacraments [*within the instituted church*].[14]

What is the Office of the Keys [which keys are found in and exercised by the instituted church]?

The preaching of the holy Gospel and Church discipline [which are exercised by the instituted church and profitable to members of the instituted church]; by which two things the kingdom of heaven is opened to believers and shut against unbelievers.[15]

How is the kingdom of heaven shut and opened by Church discipline [by the instituted church and with regard to those who are members of the instituted church, and only members of the instituted church]?

14. Heidelberg Catechism, Q&A 65, in ibid., 3:328.
15. Heidelberg Catechism, Q&A 83, in ibid., 3:337.

In this way: that, according to the command of Christ, if any under the Christian name show themselves unsound either in doctrine or life, and after repeated brotherly admonition refuse to turn from their errors or evil ways, they are complained of to the Church or to its proper officers, and, if they neglect to hear them also, are by them excluded from the holy Sacraments and the Christian communion, and by God himself from the kingdom of Christ; and if they promise and show real amendment, they are again received as members of Christ and his Church [*that is, the instituted church—the church that exercises discipline*].[16]

According to Question and Answer 85 of the Catechism, the local congregation is Christ's church. Membership in her is membership "of Christ" not for all who are on the rolls of the institute, but for true, penitent believers and their spiritual children. Whereas for the critics of *Bound to Join*, living apart from the institute is a privilege of saints or at least a legitimate option, for the Reformed creed exclusion from the institute is to be shut out from the "Christian communion" and from "the kingdom of Christ."

The Catechism's description of the church institute as the kingdom of Christ implies that just as the local congregation is the manifestation of the universal body and bride of Christ, so also is it the visible form of the kingdom of Christ in the world. Whoever esteems the kingdom of Christ will esteem the church institute. Whoever neglects or rejects the church institute by this very fact neglects or rejects the kingdom of Christ. Whoever is outside the church institute is outside the kingdom of Christ, as a rule.

Not to prolong this part of my response to criticism of *Bound to Join*, I beseech the Reformed critics of the book to consider what

16. Heidelberg Catechism, Q&A 85, in ibid., 3:337–38.

the Belgic Confession has to say about the instituted church, about the means of grace that are administered and enjoyed in the local congregation, and about the necessity, therefore, of membership in the institute. Thus the Belgic Confession refutes their criticism of the thrust of *Bound to Join*.

By means of the pastors, elders, and deacons *of the instituted church*, "true religion [is] preserved, and the true doctrine every where propagated, likewise transgressors punished and restrained by spiritual means; also that the poor and distressed may be relieved and comforted, according to their necessities."[17]

By the sacraments, which God has "joined to the word of the gospel" *in the church institute*, God "works inwardly in our hearts, thereby assuring and confirming in us the salvation which he imparts to us [by the preaching of the word and the sacraments]."[18]

From the true church, which shows itself a true church by the three marks of the preaching of the pure doctrine of the gospel, the pure administration of the sacraments, and the exercise of church discipline, "no man has a right to separate himself."[19] If no man has a right to separate himself from the true institute, no man professing faith in Christ has a right to be or remain separate from the instituted church.

"Out of it [*the instituted church displaying the three marks of the true church*] there is no salvation."[20]

I remind the critics who are content, or determined, to live apart from the instituted church of what they are lacking, or in some cases what they despise and reject. They lack the preaching of the pure doctrine of the gospel—the living voice of Jesus Christ, speaking peace to his people. They lack the sacraments—mighty instruments

17. Belgic Confession, Article 30, in ibid., 3:421–22.
18. Belgic Confession, Article 33, in ibid., 3:424.
19. Belgic Confession, Article 29, in ibid., 3:419–20.
20. Belgic Confession, Article 28, in ibid., 3:418.

of the confirmation of faith and of the increase of holiness. They lack
the oversight of elders—necessary means of Christ's watchful, shep-
herd's care of his sheep, prone always to wander.

They lack, do these critics of *Bound to Join*, the participation in
the compassionate Christ's ministry of mercy to the poor in the office of the diaconate. Private giving is not the same, no matter how
liberal. The office of the deacon in the instituted church is Christ's
official care of the poor, to which all the members are called to contribute. One may give in Christ's name *in addition to* his giving by
means of the diaconate. One may not give to the poor in Christ's
name in despite of and apart from the office of the deacons.

They lack the communion of saints. They forgo the close fellowship of the people of God, who do in fact share one spirit and one
life. They deprive themselves of the help of those who love them
with the love of God in Christ—support in the struggles and battles;
comfort in sorrow; friendship in loneliness; rebuke when they stray;
restoration when they repent; encouragement in their calling to confess Christ and walk in his ways; and a beneficial share in the talents
and gifts of all the other members in all kinds of ways.

What these neglectors and despisers of the local congregation
forget too is that communion of the saints is not only a rich gift
that one gratefully receives, but also a calling, which one dutifully
performs. The communion of saints requires every believer actively
to use his gifts for the advantage of other members: "The communion of saints [means]…that each one must feel himself bound
to use his gifts, readily and cheerfully, for the advantage and welfare of other members."[21] No one who professes Christ may live
in splendid, self-absorbed independency, selfishly concentrating on
his own spiritual welfare and, perhaps, that of his own family. For
him the body of Christ is no larger than himself and his flesh and
blood. Some body!

21. Heidelberg Catechism, Q&A 55, in ibid., 3:325.

The Precept and Privilege of Public Worship

Most important of all, sufficient by itself to move the believer to join a true church, though it costs everything and requires moving across the world and not merely across one country, those who find themselves outside the true, instituted church of Christ lack participation in the public worship of God on the Lord's day.

Participation in the public worship of God with the instituted church (of which one is a member), especially on the Christian Sabbath, is God's requirement of every believer in the fourth commandment of his law.

What does God require in the fourth commandment?
    In the first place, that the ministry of the Gospel and schools be maintained; and that I, especially on the day of rest, diligently attend church, to learn the Word of God, to use the holy Sacraments, to call publicly upon the Lord, and to give Christian alms.[22]

No private worship in his home by one who rejects or neglects membership in an instituted congregation satisfies the requirement of the fourth commandment, as is perfectly obvious from the Catechism's mention of the ministry of the gospel, attending church, learning the word of God from the ministry of the gospel, use of the sacraments, calling publicly upon the Lord, and giving Christian alms.

Neglect or rejection of membership in the instituted church is disobedience to the fourth commandment—one of the commandments belonging to the first table of the law.

The public worship of God with the worshiping congregation is

---

22. Heidelberg Catechism, Q&A 103, in ibid., 3:345.

the believer's highest calling, strongest desire, and greatest pleasure. It is this that Calvin emphasizes in his powerful polemic against the "Nicodemites" in France, who professed to be Reformed, although they were not members of a true institute and in some cases worshiped (merely outwardly as they excused themselves) with the Roman Catholic Church.

I notice that none of the critics of *Bound to Join* who are presently in view say anything at all about Calvin's condemnation of the Nicodemites, even though *Bound to Join* quotes Calvin at length and contends that its admonition is exactly the same as that given by Calvin to the Nicodemites. About Calvin, whom they claim to revere, they are silent. They protest only against *Bound to Join* and abuse only its author.

How honest this is on their part, I let every reader judge. This is what Calvin wrote to those in France who were not worshiping in a true (Reformed) institute—a passage I quote in full in *Bound to Join*.

> The third sermon [which Calvin was preaching in the particular anti-Nicodemite writing in which this quotation of Calvin is found] is to expound what a treasure it is to have freedom, not only to serve God purely and to make public confession of one's faith, but also to be in a well ordered and governed church, where the word of God is preached, and where the sacraments are properly administered, since these are the means by which God's children may be confirmed in the faith and are stirred up to live and die in his obedience. Now, it seemed to me that this point was very needful in our day, because there are many fanciful Christians who mock those who take pains to get to foreign and far off countries in order to enjoy such freedom.
>
> However, many are prevented from pursuing this bless-

ing that God esteems so highly, by their excessive regard for ease and comfort, or their fear and suspicion that they may come to lack something.[23]

Later in the same "sermon," Calvin wrote, as the expression of the sentiments of every Christian man and woman: "Lord, thou knowest how I cherish being in thy church above every worldly good."[24]

Such quotations of Calvin, insisting that the greatest of all callings of the child of God is the public worship of God as a member of the instituted church and that this calling must motivate those who are outside the instituted church to do whatever is necessary to become a member of a true institute, could be multiplied many times. In fact, many more such passages are quoted in *Bound to Join*.

Regarding the practice of some of these critics of attending the public services of churches that are charismatic in their doctrine, Arminian in their preaching, "progressive" in their liturgy, and Baptist in their covenant (mis)conception and sacramental (mal)practice, because these are the only churches available in the places where the critics live, it is to be condemned out of hand. These are false churches, according to the marks of the false church that the Belgic Confession lists in Article 29, in agreement with all the Reformed and Presbyterian creeds. The worship of these churches is not acceptable to God, indeed, is abomination to him. Those who participate make themselves guilty of the false doctrine, the impure "will-worship" (Col. 2:23), and the corruption of the sacrament.

Both because some charge that I err in condemning the membership in a Baptist church of one who confesses the Reformed faith and

23. John Calvin, *Come Out from Among Them: 'Anti-Nicodemite' Writings of John Calvin*, trans. Seth Skolnitsky (Dallas, TX: Protestant Heritage Press, 2001), 130–31, quoted in *Bound to Join*, 38–39.

24. Calvin, *Come Out from Among Them*, 188, quoted in *Bound to Join*, 52.

because of the movement today that advocates "house church" as a legitimate substitute for the instituted church, I quote Calvin on the significance of infant baptism in the matter of one's church membership. In his writing against the Nicodemites, responding to professing Reformed believers who defended their life in France outside the instituted church, Calvin said this.

> Are they at all allowed to honour God in their households? One need go no further [than their home to see]. If a child is born to one of them, it is his duty to offer him to God with prayers and thanksgiving, asking that his body be marked with the sign of salvation by baptism. Well, we know that baptism is so corrupted in the papacy, and so jumbled up with superstitions and nonsense, that a child cannot receive it without being polluted. Thus, a father would not be able to have his child baptized without sinning. If he forgoes it, it will still be sinning, and the offence is only rejecting the sacrament that the Son of God has instituted.[25]

One powerful reason that every Reformed father must be a member of an instituted church, according to Calvin, is the necessity of the baptism of his children. Christ calls the believing father to have his child baptized. But only the church institute can administer the sacrament.

The institute may not be a false church. To present one's child for baptism in a false church is sin.

For a father to refuse or fail to have his child baptized, as is necessarily the case if the father is not a member of the church institute, is grave sin: "If he forgoes it [the baptism of his infant], it will still be sinning, and the offence is only rejecting the sacrament that the Son

25. Calvin, *Come Out from Among Them*, 203–4.

of God has instituted." "Only" in the sentence is Calvinian irony.

Necessary for every believer, membership in the instituted church is all the more urgent for the father of a family—membership in a church that baptizes infants.

If a father is not a member of an instituted church, he *cannot* have his child baptized. He sins.

If a father is a member of a Baptist church, he *may not* have his child baptized. He sins.

This is my response to the critics of *Bound to Join* who willfully neglect church membership and even reject the instituted church of Jesus Christ, contentedly living outside any institute—at ease outside of God's New Testament Zion.

There are also those, although few in number, who find themselves in well-nigh impossible circumstances with regard to joining a true church. They do not angrily strike out against the instruction and admonition of *Bound to Join*, but rather desire with all their heart to worship God with a true church and cry out to God daily that he will make a way for them to join a true church. Calvin recognized such persons in France in his day. He mentioned the mother with children whose husband was an unbeliever, for whom emigration to Geneva was virtually impossible.

To such persons, *Bound to Join* gave this (pastoral) counsel, following Calvin: "Sigh and groan to God on behalf of [your] plight and for his gift to [you] and [your] children of a true church."[26]

26. Engelsma, *Bound to Join*, 75.

CHAPTER TWO

Criticism by Presbyterian Kevin Reed:
Distorting Calvin

THE CRITICISM of *Bound to Join* by Presbyterian author and publisher Kevin Reed is in basic agreement with the criticism that has been considered in the preceding chapter. Reed too takes issue with the doctrine of the Belgic Confession that there is no salvation outside the church institute. Like those who are at ease outside of God's New Testament Zion, Reed denies that membership in the instituted church is necessary. He is not "bound to join." Therefore, much of the response to the criticism of *Bound to Join* in the preceding chapter applies as well to the criticism raised by Kevin Reed.

Nevertheless, because Mr. Reed has published a lengthy attack on *Bound to Join* in which he offers specific criticisms that are supposed to refute the book's message, it is necessary to respond to Reed's criticism in a separate chapter.

Evidently, Kevin Reed takes the book *Bound to Join* seriously. He has written a twenty-one-page "review, with commentary" of the book. The review is titled "Church Membership in an Age of Idolatry and Confusion: A review, with commentary, upon *Bound to Join: Letters on Church Membership*, by David Engelsma."

Reed's criticism of *Bound to Join* is ironic—and unexpected—because he is the publisher of Calvin's book against the Nicodemites,

Come Out from Among Them, which *Bound to Join* praises highly and quotes extensively.

Reed's criticism of *Bound to Join* is given publicity in the Reformed community by the Trinity Foundation, which publishes the critical review on its website, trinityfoundation.org.

Trinity Foundation is highly regarded in certain conservative Presbyterian circles. In the past it has published Herman Hoeksema's critique of the controversy between Cornelius van Til and Gordon Clark. When Dr. John Robbins headed the organization, its magazine, *Trinity Review*, published articles of mine.

The Criticisms

Mr. Reed lists three criticisms of *Bound to Join*: "distortions regarding Calvin's treatises"; "inaccuracies regarding church history"; and "neglect of the collective teaching of the Reformation creeds."[1]

Three things are obvious about these criticisms. First, they are vague. Any critic who is unhappy with someone's position might safely charge "distortions," "inaccuracies" regarding the vast and controversial subject of church history, and "neglect of the collective teaching of the Reformation creeds" (which, it should be noted, is not the same as violation of a specific article of a particular creed). Although Mr. Reed devotes some twenty pages to a general discussion of his criticisms, never does he become specific concerning them.

---

1. Kevin Reed, "Church Membership in an Age of Idolatry and Confusion: A review, with commentary, upon *Bound to Join: Letters on Church Membership*, by David Engelsma," http://www.trinityfoundation. org/journal.php?id=279. Rather than give the further references to this article in footnotes, I will place the page number of the quotation in parentheses at the end of the quotation or reference.

Never does he state, for example, "*This* is Engelsma's distortion of Calvin, and *this* in contrast is what Calvin actually taught."

Second, the charges are not serious. They do not address the life-and-death matter treated and urged by *Bound to Join*: salvation in the church institute. At most, they amount to the charge that Engelsma is a poor scholar; perhaps, in view of the "distortions," a deceitful one. This reflects badly on the author of the book; it does not touch the book's fundamental affirmations.

Third, the criticisms carefully avoid addressing that which is at the very heart of *Bound to Join* and its message: the declaration of the Belgic Confession in Article 28 that outside the church institute is no salvation and that, therefore, every believer, including Mr. Kevin Reed, is bound to join a true, instituted church of Christ. No criticism, whether twenty pages or two hundred pages, that avoids addressing this creedal doctrine, indeed this explicit, creedal *statement*, carries any weight against *Bound to Join*, regardless that its author is a poor scholar and a liar besides.

So weak are the criticisms and such are some of Reed's statements in his review that my first impression was that the critical review is nothing more than a quarrel that the Presbyterian has with the author of the book and with the churches in which the author is a minister.

Having charged that *Bound to Join* distorts Calvin, Reed himself analyzes Calvin as teaching that it is the "obligation" of genuine believers to separate from the Roman Catholic Church and to "*seek fellowship within a true church* which adheres to the true Gospel and right worship" (2; emphasis is Reed's). But this is the analysis of Calvin's doctrine of church membership in *Bound to Join*.

After eighteen pages of severe criticism of *Bound to Join*, which must leave every reader with the impression that Reed differs radically with the book's understanding of the calling of believers regarding church membership, Reed offers his own view of this calling of believers.

> For a professing Christian to live in willful seclusion from
> the true church is contrary to the express teaching of Scrip-
> ture, which represents each member of the body as a mere
> part of the body in need of the whole...Sincere believers
> should join a sound Christian congregation—a church
> which exhibits the qualities stressed in the Scriptures, as
> illustrated in Reformed creeds. If there is no sound church
> in their vicinity, they should work to establish one; or they
> may also consider the option to relocate to a place where
> there is a sound congregation (19).

With the exception of the phrase "they may also consider the option to relocate," and understanding "should" as indicating duty, this
is the message of *Bound to Join*.

Why then the critical review?

Is the reason merely that Mr. Reed likes to pick a public quarrel
with the author of the book and with the churches in which he is a
member?

If this were the case, I would never respond to the criticism.

There is far more at work in the review and commentary than
only personal grudges.

Despite the weakness of his specific criticisms and their curious
avoidance of the main issue in the book against which they are lodged,
and despite the seeming approximation of Reed's understanding of
the duty of church membership to that of the book, Reed's review
is, in fact, a vigorous repudiation of the fundamental teaching of
Bound to Join. Reed denies that, because salvation is found only in
the church institute that displays the marks of the true church, every
believer is required to be a member of the church institute. Reed
defends, as a spiritual policy, the right of believers to live outside of
and apart from the church institute, and to do so for years, if not for
life. He defends this policy and corresponding practice not in some
Muslim country, where organization of a church is forbidden and

membership in a Christian church is punished with death, but in the United States, where believers may yet freely assemble for the public worship of God.

Reed takes issue with the necessity of membership in a church institute because he is an advocate and practitioner of a distinct ecclesiology—a distinct doctrine of the church. This doctrine of the church differs radically from the Reformed doctrine of the church of the Belgic Confession in Articles 27–35, as also from the doctrine of the church of John Calvin. Inasmuch as the doctrine of the church of John Calvin, of the Belgic Confession, and of the other Reformed creeds is, by the acknowledgment of all Reformed believers, the doctrine of the Bible, Mr. Reed's doctrine of the church is unbiblical.

The doctrine of the church espoused, defended, and, evidently, practiced by Kevin Reed is the "house church."

What this doctrine of the church consists of, how it plainly violates the doctrine of the church of the Reformed creeds, and that it is no church, I will demonstrate later in this response.

One thing is incontrovertibly plain: by defending the house church against the church institute, Mr. Reed contradicts Article 28 of the Belgic Confession. Of the *instituted* church, not a house church, Article 28 of the Reformed confession states, "Out of it there is no salvation." Therefore, according to this article of the creed, "No person of whatsoever state or condition he may be, ought to withdraw himself, to live in a separate state from it." Rather, "all men are in duty bound to join and unite themselves with it."

Such is the necessity of membership in the church institute, according to the Belgic Confession, that all believers must "join themselves to this congregation, wheresoever God hath established it, even though the magistrates and edicts of princes be against it; yea, though they should suffer death or bodily punishment." The conclusion is: "Therefore all those who separate themselves from the same, or do not join themselves to it, act contrary to the ordinance of God."[2]

It is his adherence to the doctrine of house church that moved Kevin Reed to criticize *Bound to Join*, its author, and the churches in which the author is a minister. In actuality, his criticism falls on the Belgic Confession, as he himself at one point is compelled to acknowledge.

Because Reed's three stated criticisms of *Bound to Join*, weak and vague as they are, discredit the book's urgent admonition, and are intended to discredit that admonition, I must respond to two of them. They are the charge that the book distorts Calvin's treatises on church membership and the charge that the book neglects the "collective teaching of the Reformation creeds."

The third charge, that the book contains "inaccuracies regarding church history," I ignore, not because the charge is true, but because it is irrelevant. *Bound to Join* does not appeal to church history. It appeals to the Reformed creeds, specifically, the Belgic Confession. Whatever conclusions Mr. Reed elicits from his reading of church history are without weight in the discussion. Not Reed's understanding of church history but the creeds are authoritative among Reformed and Presbyterian persons.

Reed's charges against *Bound to Join* are false.

That Reed dares to make these charges is evidence that he does not know the readership of *Bound to Join*, mainly Protestant Reformed people, but also other Reformed and Presbyterian persons who are deeply concerned about the Reformed faith and life. If I had distorted the teaching of Calvin on church membership, particularly in his book *Come Out from Among Them* (which I recommend in *Bound to Join* to all the readers), and if I failed accurately to present

2. Belgic Confession, Article 28, in Schaff, *Creeds of Christendom*, 3:418–19.

the testimony of the Reformed creeds, the readers of *Bound to Join* would have indignantly called this to my attention, dismissed the book, and likely called for public recantation.

Even if I were not motivated by the fundamental Christian virtue of honesty (which must govern the writing of books, as well as all other discourse), the certain testing of my writing by the readers, many of whom have carefully read Calvin's *Come Out from Among Them* and all of whom are thoroughly familiar with the three forms of unity, if not also with the Westminster standards, would have required me to do my homework in Calvin and the creeds and to present their doctrine of the church correctly.

Distortion

A careful reading of Reed's screed shows that my alleged distortions of Calvin's teaching in *Come Out from Among Them* are two. Both have to do with Calvin's instruction of Reformed believers in France who were required by the civil authorities to participate in the public worship of the Roman Catholic Church. Some of them were taking part in Roman Catholic worship, merely outwardly, as they said, because of the very real threat of persecution.

The first alleged distortion is my contention that Calvin's main concern was that these professing Reformed believers worship God rightly in a true, instituted church. According to Reed, Calvin's main concern was only that these Reformed people not participate in the corrupt worship of Rome.

Reed writes:

> It was not primarily a matter of church membership that
> moved Calvin to rebut the Nicodemites, but their will-
> ingness to participate in acts of Romish idolatry, [and]
> to behave deceptively in their general profession…Thus,
> we must avoid placing a disproportionate stress upon the

subject of church membership, as Professor Engelsma does, thereby distorting Calvin's true emphasis.

At no point does Calvin frame his discussion as a treatise on church membership. While it may be valid to derive implications respecting church membership from Calvin's expositions, it is a distortion to use the reformer's "Anti-Nicodemite" writings as if they were a diatribe [*sic*] on church membership—missing the reformer's main emphases on genuine piety, sincere confession, and right worship (2).

A little later, Reed repeats the charge: "Professor Engelsma's stress on church membership leaves the impression that Calvin is obsessed [*sic*] about church membership" (5).

Reed's correction of this alleged distortion of Calvin is twofold. Reed maintains that Calvin's chief concern was that the Reformed believers in France not worship with Rome. With regard to Calvin's secondary concern, namely, that the Reformed believers in France worship God rightly, Calvin (according to Kevin Reed) was satisfied that those believers would worship God *outside the church institute* in private gatherings in their homes.

Let us examine both aspects of Reed's correction of the first alleged distortion of Calvin by *Bound to Join*. (I ignore Reed's pejorative language—"diatribe," "obsessed," and a number of other derogatory and inflammatory terms; it detracts from a serious consideration of a great truth.)

The first aspect of Reed's correction, namely, that Calvin was primarily concerned that the Reformed believers separate from Roman Catholic worship, and only secondarily that they worship God rightly, is as foolish as it is false. To suppose that Calvin was more concerned that Reformed believers not worship God falsely than that they worship God rightly is to suppose that for Calvin it is more important that we have no other gods than that we have the one, true God as God.

For Calvin, in the book *Come Out from Among Them*, the main concern was that the Reformed believers worship God rightly. Indeed, his concern that they separate from the corrupt worship of Rome had as its purpose, its goal, its ultimate reason, that they worship God rightly. Separation from Rome would be meaningless and worthless if it did not end in the right worship of God, indeed, if it were not *motivated* by the desire to worship God rightly.

Calvin understood that the first commandment of the law forbids idolatry not as an end in itself, but in the interests of the worship of the one, true God. Calvin made plain to the Nicodemites in France that his purpose in forbidding them to participate in the Roman Catholic mass was that they celebrate the Lord's supper rightly in a true, instituted church. On the basis of the apostolic teaching in 1 Corinthians 10:21, Calvin did not simply say to the Nicodemites, "You may not drink the cup of devils; you may not be partakers of the table of devils." But he said, "Ye cannot drink the cup of the Lord, and the cup of devils: ye cannot be partakers of the Lord's table, and of the table of devils." Calvin's primary concern was that the French believers *drink the cup of the Lord* and *partake of the Lord's table*. And this requires that believers be members of the church institute.

Calvin expressed his main concern in all his anti-Nicodemite writings in his introduction to the four sermons that make up a large part of the book *Come Out from Among Them*. In the sermons, as in all his admonitions to the professing Reformed believers in France, Calvin set forth "the doctrine of worshipping God purely." Especially the third sermon expounded "what a treasure it is to have freedom...to serve God purely and to make public confession of one's faith." The fourth sermon extolled "the privilege of hearing the word of God preached purely, of calling upon his name and enjoying the sacraments." Calvin's exposition of Psalm 87 was apt "because it deals with the restoration of the church of God."[3]

The first of the four sermons had Psalm 16:4 as its text. The text is negative: "Their drink offerings of blood will I not offer, nor take up their names into my lips." Calvin applied the text to the calling of Reformed believers to separate from Roman Catholic worship. But even in his sermon on the negative text, Calvin made plain that his main concern was that the Nicodemites worship God rightly. "It accomplishes nothing to turn from an accustomed evil to other counterfeits; rather, superstitions must be abolished altogether, so that the true religion may be established in its purity. For otherwise, men do not come directly to God."[4]

In the same sermon, Calvin insisted that the desire to worship God rightly must be the motivation for abandoning Roman Catholic worship:

> What then should we do? In all of this there is a certain
> goal we must aim for: let the zeal of God's house tug at
> our hearts…When such a zeal burns in our hearts, not
> for a bit, but unceasingly, we will care so little whether we
> are permitted to pretend to approve abominations which
> dishonour God…Note carefully what was said, 'the zeal of
> God's house' [Ps. 69:9].[5]

Important as it was to Calvin that Reformed Christians in France not participate in Roman Catholic worship, that was not his main purpose with his anti-Nicodemite writings. His main purpose, he expressed in these words: "Let every man draw aside with his own

3. Calvin, *Come Out from Among Them*, 130–31.
4. Ibid., 148.
5. Ibid., 150–51.

conscience, address God and say, 'Lord, thou knowest how I cherish being in thy church above every worldly good.'"[6]

By "church" in this last quotation and throughout the book *Come Out from Among Them*, Calvin meant a congregation instituted in the three special offices of pastor, elder, and deacon. Calvin's main concern, therefore, was church membership.

This is the second aspect of Reed's charge that I distort Calvin's teaching by presenting it as an urgent call to the Nicodemites to worship God in a true church institute. Not only do I err in *Bound to Join* by affirming that Calvin's main concern was the right worship of God, but I also err in insisting that Calvin had in mind right worship *in an instituted church*.

House Church

According to Kevin Reed, Calvin was satisfied with the private worship of God by a family in their home or, preferably, by several families in the home of one of them. Indeed, according to Mr. Reed, this is all that Calvin intended in the anti-Nicodemite writings when he urged the French believers to worship God rightly in the church.

Here we come to the real issue in the controversy Kevin Reed instigated against *Bound to Join*. Reed defends a radically different doctrine of the church from that urged by *Bound to Join*, and from that of the Belgic Confession, which *Bound to Join* exhorts. For Mr. Reed, a church is an unorganized gathering of a family and as many others as will join them for private worship in a home on the Lord's day. This is Reed's house church.

House church, for Kevin Reed and a growing number of others today, is *not* a church that meets in a house, that is, a congregation with the offices of pastor, elder, and deacon that, because of its small size and its desire to save money, meets in a house. Churches of

6. Ibid., 188.

Christ have often met in houses. They have also met in catacombs, in the fields, and, for that matter, in theaters that were rented for the worship service. Where it meets is not fundamental to the church. What is fundamental is that the gathering is instituted.

But a house church is a gathering for worship especially of a family in its house, although others are welcome. The gathering is not instituted. There is no office of pastor, no office of elder, and no office of deacon. The service of worship in the house is under the direction of the husband and father of the family. The gathering is not the church institute. It is a house church.

In his sharp criticism of *Bound to Join*, Reed is not candid about his doctrine of the church. He does not define or carefully describe the house church that he obviously is defending against the church institute that *Bound to Join* insists on. Reed merely assures us that "where there is no regular congregation, there is the prospect of meeting with others in homes, as a means of reconstituting a true church" (3). In a footnote, he asks, rhetorically, "Shouldn't the historic formulation of house churches and other underground assemblies…inform the meaning of the believer's duty to join himself to the true church…?" (11). Appealing to the history of the church in Scotland in the sixteenth century, Reed evidently approves of "privy kirks" in Europe and in the United States in the twenty-first century (4). "Privy kirks," apparently, would be the same as house churches.

Recognizing that Reed is defending the house church over against the church institute makes many things in his criticism of *Bound to Join* plain that otherwise are puzzling. It explains the puzzling apparent agreement of Reed with the main thrust of *Bound to Join*, when, in fact, Reed is opposed to the book. When Reed takes issue with my statement that Calvin "insists on membership in a true, instituted congregation" and immediately corrects the statement by affirming that Calvin taught that all should "*seek to worship God faithfully in a true congregation of believers*"—seemingly affirming the very thing for which he has criticized me—the explanation is that Reed has a house church in mind (6; the emphasis is Reed's).

Reed is irritated by my calling attention to Calvin's demand that the Nicodemites move to another place, even another country, where the right worship of God is possible because Reed is intent on defending the house church. If God is satisfied with private worship in a family's home, there is little, if any, need to move—ever.

Reed criticizes my insistence on the preaching of the gospel as the main means of grace (in spite of the fact that every Reformed confession teaches this, which Reed again neglects to notice). Against this insistence (by Engelsma, of course, not by the creeds, is the impression that Reed leaves) he pleads for recognizing the reading of the Bible as a means of grace. "Engelsma does not give due place to the reading of the Word as an effectual means of grace…The private reading of Scripture is a means of grace" (15).

Presbyterian husbands and fathers in their house church can read the Scripture. They are probably hesitant, this early in the house church movement, to preach. Therefore, for a defender of the house church, the reading of the Bible must be recognized as a means of grace with the preaching of the gospel, indeed, in practice, *in place of* the preaching of the gospel.

Likewise, Reed is critical of my limiting the marks of the true church to preaching, sacraments, and discipline. He laments that I deny that love is a mark of the true church. Again, he ignores that every Reformed creed makes preaching and sacraments the marks of the true church, while some add discipline, and that no creed makes love a mark of the church. Reed is bold to charge that my list of the marks of the true church "obscure[s] important emphases of scripture." He adds: "When he [Engelsma] disclaims love as being too subjective to measure [as a mark of the true church], he does great disservice to the teachings of both Christ and the apostle Paul" (18). One can make love a mark of the church, if by "church" he has in mind an unorganized gathering of family and friends—a house church—and if he is determined to disregard the Reformed confessions.

Keeping in mind that church for Reed is a house church also explains his disjunction between right worship, on the one hand, and church membership, on the other. "For Calvin, as well as Knox, church membership, *per se*, is not the driving factor: *the Gospel and proper worship are the preeminent issues*" (5). Proper worship of believers on the Lord's day is possible apart from church membership, in the ecclesiology of Kevin Reed. According to Mr. Reed, believers may, *and can*, worship God properly apart from the church institute in a house church. That is, it is both permissible and possible for believers to carry out the requirement of the fourth commandment concerning what the Heidelberg Catechism describes as diligently attending church, learning the word of God at church, using the sacraments, calling publicly upon the Lord, and giving alms *apart from the church institute.*[7]

But did John Calvin have Kevin Reed's house church in view when, in his anti-Nicodemite writings, he admonished the believers in France that they must worship God rightly in a true church? Reed thinks so. Therefore, he criticizes me for distorting Calvin when I state that Calvin exhorted the Nicodemites to worship God rightly by becoming members of a true, instituted church. "We must avoid placing a disproportionate stress upon the subject of church membership, as Professor Engelsma does, thereby distorting Calvin's true emphasis. At no point does Calvin frame his discussion as a treatise on church membership" (2).

Reed is mistaken.

This aspect too of his charge of distortion against *Bound to Join* is false.

Calvin on the Church

When Calvin called the professing Reformed Christians in

7. Heidelberg Catechism, Q&A 103, in Schaff, *Creeds of Christendom*, 3:345.

France to worship God in a true church, he meant an instituted church. Whether it met in a house or in the field or in a cave of the earth, the church in which every believer is called by God to worship, in Calvin's ecclesiology, is a gathering of believers and their children *that is organized in and by the office of the preaching of the gospel, the office of the administration of the sacraments, and the office of the exercise of discipline.* The worship that the true God requires is public, official worship by the instituted congregation. Every believer is called by God to participate in this official, public worship, especially on the Lord's day.

The ecclesiology of John Calvin was not that of Kevin Reed and the house church movement. That it was not the doctrine of the church of Kevin Reed is evident from all the Reformed creeds, which are very much dependent in this aspect of doctrine, as in all the others, upon John Calvin. None of them teaches the house church. All of them teach the instituted congregation.

But I must show that Calvin had the church institute in mind in *Come Out from Among Them,* and that I did not distort the reformer when I said so.

Calvin urged upon his Nicodemite readers in France that "the Lord Jesus indeed commands us to submit to his church…This is because it is the pillar and ground of [the] truth."[8]

No one can possibly submit to Reed's house church. It has no authority from Christ, no offices. In addition, it is of the utmost significance that Calvin appeals to 1 Timothy 3:15 in support of his exhortation ("pillar and ground of the truth"). First Timothy 3 is one of the outstanding chapters in the New Testament *on the church institute and on the necessity of membership in the church institute.* This is the chapter on the office of bishop, with its "care of the church of

---

8. Calvin, *Come Out from Among Them,* 40.

God," and on the office of deacon, with its "use." The institute is the "house of God...the church of the living God, the pillar and ground of the truth" (1 Tim. 3:15).

And, let it be emphatically noted, the institute (according to the correct translation of 1 Timothy 3:16) makes, and maintains, the great confession of the truth of the gospel of Jesus Christ in the world: "Confessedly, great is the mystery of godliness..."

Again and again, Calvin held before the professing Reformed Christians in France the necessity of being members of an "ordered" church, indeed, of a "rightly-ordered church." "All those who are in a country where there is no manner of rightly-ordered church where they can worship God and call upon him (and hear his word and enjoy his sacraments) ought indeed to sigh with Daniel."[9] According to Calvin, the "main [means]" by which the believer "aspire[s] to God's heavenly kingdom" is "the order and policy which God has established in his church."[10] Calvin continued: "So, we should be clear on the high esteem he [David in Psalm 27:4] has for the outward order which directs the faithful in the church."[11] Calvin warns sharply against despising the "preaching of the gospel and...the sacraments *as of the rest of the church order.*"[12] Like David in Psalm 27:8, Calvin considered "how necessary the order of the church is to all mortal men."[13]

What this "order" or "right order" of the church is Calvin made clear in virtually every context in which he spoke of the order of the church. It is the order of the exercise and use of the three special offices of preacher of the gospel, or pastor, ruling elder, and deacon.

9. Ibid., 123.
10. Ibid., 177–78.
11. Ibid., 179.
12. Ibid., 200; emphasis added.
13. Ibid., 206. 123; emphasis added.

The "rightly-ordered church" is that assembly of the people of God where believers and their children "can worship God and call upon him (*and hear his word and enjoy his sacraments*)."[14]

To one living where he "may not worship God purely," Calvin's "first advice" was to leave for "a place where he…[is permitted] to profess his Christianity in the assembly of Christians, to be a partaker of the holy doctrine of the gospel, to enjoy the pure and entire use of the sacraments, and to share in the public prayers."[15]

The "order and policy which God has established in his church" is this: "that we be taught by his word, that we all worship him of one accord, and that we call upon him, having the observance of the sacraments to help us do this."[16]

To those who, like Kevin Reed, "do not deign to maintain the ranks…through the common order of the church," Calvin answered, "in the first place, that the need to be taught through sermons, to be confirmed through the sacraments, and trained in public prayers and confessing the faith, is common to us and the ancient fathers."[17]

The church that Calvin exhorted upon the Nicodemites was the church in which there is "the teaching of the gospel, when it is preached, the sacraments, when they are rightly practiced, [and] public prayer."[18]

So clear, emphatic, and repeated is Calvin's insistence in *Come Out from Among Them* that believers must have membership in the church institute, that one is inclined to suppose that Kevin Reed, who denies that Calvin was talking about the church institute and who charges me with distortion of Calvin for affirming Calvin's insistence on membership in the church institute, never read Calvin's book. But Reed is the publisher of Calvin's book.

14. Ibid., 123; emphasis added.
15. Ibid., 93–94.
16. Ibid., 178.
17. Ibid., 182.
18. Ibid., 207.

What the explanation may be of Reed's charge against me of distortion of Calvin at this point is not for me to judge.

What is important, and incontrovertible, is that Calvin's doctrine of the church was that an assembly of believers and their children is a church by virtue, and *only* by virtue, of the ordering or instituting of the assembly by the three special offices of pastor, elder, and deacon. The church is the assembly that preaches the gospel *through the office of pastor and teacher in the assembly*. The church is the assembly that governs itself *through the office of ruling elder in the assembly*. The church is the assembly that administers the mercies of Christ *through the office of deacon in the assembly*.

This assembly worships God publicly with the worship on the Lord's day required in the fourth commandment. Every believer is called by God to worship him diligently *as a member of this assembly, that is, the church institute*. Every believer is called by God to worship him, as a member of this assembly, *by hearing the preaching through the office of pastor, by submitting to the rule of Christ through the office of elder, and by contributing to, or using, as the case may be, the alms through the office of deacon*.

Calvin on Church Membership

Of the church institute—the church that preaches, rules, and administers alms—every believer is required by God to be a member, according to Calvin.

Some, including Kevin Reed, have criticized me, and none too kindly, for my strong language in insisting on the necessity of church membership. Reed suggests that "Engelsma's exhortations are intended to…brow-beat persons into submission to the Protestant Reformed Churches' extra-Scriptural impositions in worship" (17). Evidently, Reed did not notice that he reacts to my admonitions about the necessity of the right worship of God in the church institute exactly as some of the Nicodemites reacted to Calvin's similar admonitions. Calvin took note of "those babblers who ridicule us, wondering if one cannot get to paradise except by way of Geneva."[19]

In fact, my language in *Bound to Join* was deliberately restrained, in comparison with the forcefulness of Calvin's language. My restraint was not due to disagreement with Calvin's vehemence. It was tactical. I wanted *Bound to Join* to get a hearing in this hyper-sensitive, soft-soaping age. But now my critics, particularly Mr. Reed, will listen to Calvin on the necessity of membership in a true church institute.

"How necessary the order of the church is to all mortal men."[20]

"The blessing of being part of the flock of God under the outward order and direction that he has established" is and must be esteemed a "good...above all others."[21]

With appeal to Ephesians 4:11, which refers to the "order of the church as Jesus Christ instituted it when he gave pastors," Calvin declares, "Cursed be the nonchalance of those who want to flit about in the air, and pretend to climb to heaven by means of their own speculations, despising sermons and the use of the sacraments."[22]

Those who think that "sermons, public prayers and the sacraments are superfluous for them" are "prideful men."[23]

"No one is of the body of Christ, nor should be so accounted, unless he submits to this general rule (Eph. 4:4)," that is, "taught through sermons...confirmed through the sacraments, and trained in public prayers and confessing the faith."[24]

Those who do not "feel their ill and wretchedness" outside the church institute, where is the "use of the sacraments," are "more stupid than the dumb beasts."[25]

---

19. Ibid., 192.
20. Ibid., 206.
21. Ibid., 187.
22. Ibid., 191.
23. Ibid., 181.
24. Ibid., 182.
25. Ibid., 184.

People who are content with not being "preached to," "never partake [of the supper]," and "consign…to little children" the "outward order of the church" are "beyond blind," even though they are not worshiping with the papists.[26]

"Those who despise the usage of which I speak [namely, the preaching of the gospel], as much of the sacraments as of the rest of the church order, do not deign to behold God when he appears to them."[27]

And those who complain about Calvin's rigor, both in requiring that they separate from false worship and in commanding them to worship God rightly in a true church, as though Calvin "were too extreme" (a familiar complaint), are "big babies."[28]

This is my response to the first false charge by Presbyterian Kevin Reed that I distorted Calvin in *Bound to Join*. My only distortion, if such it was, was that I did not do full justice to the vehemence of Calvin's admonition that all believers must join a true, instituted church of Christ. I have now corrected this error.

Calvin on Moving

Reed's second, related charge of distortion concerns my presentation of Calvin in *Come Out from Among Them* as urging the French believers to leave France, if necessary leaving all things earthly behind, in order to become members of true churches in other lands. In keeping with this admonition by Calvin, in *Bound to Join* I urged Reformed believers in similar circumstances to move from one place to another, if necessary from one country to another, in order to become members of a true church of Christ.

Reed charges distortion.

26. Ibid., 191.
27. Ibid., 200.
28. Ibid., 142.

> In this argument for relocation, Engelsma glosses Calvin's
> writings claiming, "Calvin called the French Reformed
> to leave all behind and come to Geneva," again speaking
> of "Calvin's exhortation to leave France in order to join
> the true church"…Neither Calvin's text nor the historical
> evidence supports this gloss (6– 7).

No one may suppose that I exhorted moving hastily or rashly.
Moving for the sake of membership in a true church, especially from
one country to another, is a last resort, taken only after exploring
every other possibility and when it is evident that such membership
is impossible in one's native land. This was the situation of the Nicodemites to whom Calvin addressed the writings that are the content
of *Come Out from Among Them.*

I wrote:

> Those who find themselves outside a true church with none
> in the immediate area must either work hard at establish-
> ing a true church in the area with like-minded Christians
> or, if this proves impossible, move to a place where there is
> a true church.

I added: "Calvin called the French Reformed to leave all behind
and come to Geneva."[29]

That Calvin called the French Reformed to leave France and, if
necessary, all their earthly possessions and move to another country
in order to worship God rightly in a true church was not my false
and misleading interpretation of Calvin's anti-Nicodemite writings
(this is the meaning of "gloss"). It is "Calvin's text."

At the very beginning of his "A Short Treatise Setting Forth
What the Faithful Man Must Do When He is Among Papists and

---

29. Engelsma, *Bound to Join,* 71–72.

He Knows the Truth of the Gospel," Calvin wrote: "I grant that it is a hard thing to put oneself in danger of losing body and goods…of leaving the land where one can live comfortably in order to depart for a strange land, like someone lost."[30] Calvin was calling the Nicodemites to leave their land, and he told them so.

Later in the same "Short Treatise," Calvin gave his counsel to the believer who was living in a land "where he may not worship God purely, but is forced by the common practice to accommodate himself to bad things": "The first advice would be to leave if he could."[31]

More perceptive than Kevin Reed, the Nicodemites responded to Calvin's instruction concerning the necessity of church membership with the question, "What!…Shall we all depart to run away to an unknown place?"[32]

Understanding full well that the implication of Calvin's instruction concerning the necessity of church membership was that they must leave France for a country where the right worship of God was possible, the Nicodemites responded, "What would happen if all the faithful determined to flee idolatry? The lands in which God has a great seed [particularly, France] would become deserts."[33]

Calvin rebuked those who argued against his admonitions about church membership by appealing to their duty toward their rulers: "Some point out that they may not lawfully leave the land of their birth…because of the duty they have to their earthly prince." Calvin responded that these same people would leave in a hurry if they had no food or drink, or if there was the prospect of earthly riches in a foreign land. "If they were offered six times as many goods in a foreign country, they would have no great problem leaving promptly to

30. Calvin, *Come Out from Among Them*, 48.
31. Ibid., 93.
32. Ibid., 111.
33. Ibid., 115.

take possession."[34] It is clear that "Calvin's text" to the French believers was that they should move and that they knew it.

Because the public worship of God in an instituted church is necessary—not merely an "option," as is the thinking of Kevin Reed—Calvin taught that a believing husband ought to leave his home and country for the sake of membership in a true, instituted church, even though he must leave his wife behind.

> The husband must point out to his wife how unhappy they are being separated from the company of the faithful, having neither preaching [not the reading of the Bible, but preaching], nor sacraments [in a church institute therefore], which are the signs to assure us that God is dwelling with us. He thereupon urges her to summon her courage, and if he cannot win her over as quickly as he would like, he does not weary [of persuading her] until he gets the job done. Even if the wife disagrees with him, let him not stop persisting with her until she shows herself altogether obstinate. If after having done all he can, he can no longer stand it there, he is free and clear; he has acquitted himself of his duty and has not clung to her, because his wife did not follow him as she is bound to do. However, such a parting is not a divorce. Rather, the husband goes ahead to show his wife the way.[35]

It will be difficult to convince one who has read this section of Calvin's anti-Nicodemite writings that *Bound to Join* is "glossing" Calvin when it explains Calvin as teaching the necessity of membership in a true church, even though this requires one to leave his country.[36]

---

34. Ibid., 202.
35. Ibid., 205.
36. See ibid., 205–6.

The problem regarding "Calvin's text" on the necessity of church membership was not that it failed to make clear that moving would be required. Rather, the problem was that wicked men "ridicule those who go to a foreign country to seek and enjoy" the blessings of church membership, namely, "sermons, public prayers and the sacraments."[37]

If only those in places where membership in a true church is impossible would have impressed upon their hearts "to come to a Christian church where they can die in peace, everyone would soon have his bag packed."[38] To those in a place where membership in a true church is impossible, Calvin's exhortation was, "Pack your bags!"

Bound to Join did not distort Calvin's anti-Nicodemite writings. Calvin taught the necessity of membership in a true, instituted church, even though joining would require leaving one's country, leaving one's possessions, and leaving one's family.

In *Bound to Join* I restricted myself to Calvin's teaching on church membership as this is found in his anti-Nicodemite writings. Here I may add a few, brief expressions of Calvin's high regard for the church institute and of his insistence on lively membership in the church institute from his *Institutes*.

That Calvin had the highest regard for the visible, instituted church is evident from the space devoted to it. Book 4 of the *Institutes*, which is mainly the doctrine of the church, gives only a few pages to the explanation of the universal, invisible church of the elect. Hundreds of pages treat of the visible institute. For Calvin, the visible institute is the assembly of believers and their children ordered in the offices, especially the office of preaching and sacraments.

About the church institute and the necessity of membership in it, Calvin wrote the following.

37. Ibid., 181.
38. Ibid., 206.

Where the preaching of the gospel is reverently heard and the sacraments are not neglected, there for the time being no deceitful or ambiguous form of the church is seen; and no one is permitted to spurn its authority, flout its warnings, resist its counsels, or make light of its chastisements—much less to desert it and break its unity. For the Lord esteems the communion of his church so highly that he counts as a traitor and apostate from Christianity anyone who arrogantly leaves any Christian society, provided it cherishes the true ministry of Word and sacraments. He so esteems the authority of the church that when it is violated he believes his own diminished...From this it follows that separation from the church is the denial of God and Christ.[39]

[God] has...bound us to this ordinary manner of teaching [the office of the preaching of the gospel in the congregation]. Fanatical men, refusing to hold fast to it, entangle themselves in many deadly snares. Many are led either by pride, dislike, or rivalry to the conviction that they can profit enough from private reading and meditation; hence they despise public assemblies and deem preaching superfluous. But, since they do their utmost to sever or break the sacred bond of unity, no one escapes the just penalty of this unholy separation without bewitching himself with pestilent errors and foulest delusions.[40]

He who voluntarily deserts the outward communion of the church (where the Word of God is preached and the sacraments are administered) is without excuse.[41]

39. Calvin, *Institutes*, 4.1.10, 2:1024. The context of the grave warning that concludes this quotation is Calvin's explicit reference to 1 Timothy 3:15, which calls the church institute the "house of God."

40. Ibid., 4.1.5, 2:1018.

41. Ibid., 4.1.19, 2:1033.

[Christ] has...set off by plainer marks the knowledge of his very body to us, *knowing how necessary it is to our salvation...* Wherever we see the Word of God purely preached and heard, and the sacraments administered according to Christ's institution...[42]

One may disagree with Calvin. It is understandable that people do disagree with Calvin. Many did in his own day—angrily. One of Calvin's writings has the title, "Answer of John Calvin to the Nicodemite Gentlemen concerning Their Complaint that He is too Severe." The passage of Scripture that Calvin quoted on the title page is Amos 5:10: "They hate him that rebuketh in the gate, and they abhor him that speaketh uprightly."[43]

The way to the public worship of God in a true church is often difficult, requiring sacrifice and suffering. The way of *remaining* in a true church is often difficult. Calvin recognized this. Therefore, an important element of his admonitions to the Nicodemites was his reminder that discipleship after Christ requires hardship and loss. One of the sermons he sent the French believers was on Hebrews 13:13: "Let us go forth therefore unto him without the camp, bearing his reproach."[44] In another of the sermons to the Nicodemites, Calvin wrote this.

There is no trouble or hardship that we are not supposed to endure in order to enjoy the face of God. So, is it a matter of seeking a place where one has liberty to serve God and worship him purely? Whatever the hardship that lies between two points, let one not fail to set out on the journey.[45]

42. Ibid., 4.1.8–9, 2:1022–23; emphasis added.
43. Calvin, *Come Out from Among Them,* 97.
44. Ibid., 154.
45. Ibid., 212.

Calvin added that if zeal for the church of God "reigned in all believers, they would not have so much trouble disentangling themselves and would not spend so much time haggling about the loss. They must take leave of their homes and come to the church of God."[46]

The Belgic Confession likewise warns Reformed believers to count the cost of their discipleship after Christ with regard to joining, and never separating from, a true church, "*wheresoever God hath established it*": "even though the magistrates and edicts of princes be against it; yea, though they should suffer death or bodily punishment."[47]

One may disagree with Calvin's doctrine of church membership. He ought not to evade it by charging distortion against a book that presents that doctrine in its rigor.

Bound to Join does not distort Calvin. This has been proved.

---

46. Ibid., 215.

47. Belgic Confession, Article 28, in Schaff, *Creeds of Christendom*, 3:418; emphasis added.

CHAPTER THREE

⟡⟡⟡

Criticism by Presbyterian Kevin Reed: Neglecting the Creeds

NEITHER DOES the book "neglect...the collective teaching of the Reformation creeds." This is the second significant charge against *Bound to Join* by Kevin Reed in his "review, with commentary": "[*Bound to Join*] contain[s]...neglect of the collective teaching of the Reformation creeds" (1). By this charge, Mr. Reed attempts to blunt the force of the book. As its title indicates, *Bound to Join* explains and applies to all who are not members of a true, instituted church, as well as to all who are members of a true church, the declaration of the Reformed creed the Belgic Confession: "All men are in duty bound to join and unite themselves with it," that is, with the true church institute. Expressing the urgency of this "duty," the Belgic Confession states concerning this congregation that "out of it there is no salvation."[1]

Opposition to the Belgic Confession

Mr. Reed is opposed to this teaching of the Belgic Confession. He denies that all confessing believers are bound to join an instituted church that has the marks of the true church, because outside the church institute is no salvation. This is the reason for his angry attack on *Bound to Join*. Although he portrays his attack as directed against

1. Belgic Confession, Article 28, in Schaff, *Creeds of Christendom*, 3:418.

the book and its author, in fact, his attack is directed squarely against Article 28 of the Belgic Confession (and against John Calvin, whose influence upon Article 28 of the Belgic Confession is determinative).

But as a Presbyterian, Reed is loath frankly to criticize a Reformed creed, as well he might be. His tactic with regard to Article 28 of the Belgic Confession, when in his "review, with commentary" he is finally compelled to address the article, is twofold. First, he suggests that my explanation of the article as referring to the visible church institute is merely my (erroneous) "construction" on the article. That is, Article 28 does not refer to the church institute, but to the church of the elect—the "invisible church" (14). "Moreover, if the Belgic Confession bears the construction Professor Engelsma places on it…" (14–15).

But Mr. Reed himself has little hope of the success of this tactic with his Reformed readership. The language of the Belgic Confession is too clear and compelling. Therefore, the second and main tactic of Reed concerning Article 28 of the Belgic Confession is to propose that the Belgic Confession contradicts the other Reformed creeds. The Belgic Confession is in error. He continues: "…then [that is, if the Belgic Confession bears the 'construction' that Engelsma places on it] the Belgic Confession stands in contrast or contradiction to other Reformed creeds, which speak in absolute terms only with respect to the church of the elect" (14–15).

According to this analysis by Kevin Reed, the book *Bound to Join* cannot be severely faulted, not nearly as severely as Reed faults it. After all, it only promotes the error of a leading Reformed creed. The Reformed confession led the book's author astray. In fact, Reed's harsh, twenty-one-page attack on *Bound to Join* and its author is wholly misdirected. The Belgic Confession deserves the criticism.

In reality, the matter stands thus: In the interests of his dear house church, Kevin Reed is willing to oppose the ecclesiology—the doctrine of the church—of the Belgic Confession. And opposing the doctrine of the Belgic Confession, he opposes the doctrine of the church of all the Reformation confessions. Because the Reformed confessions present Scripture's doctrine of the church, as all Reformed believers have affirmed, Reed is found opposing the biblical doctrine of the church.

Both aspects of Reed's tactic in handling Article 28 of the Belgic Confession are false.

First, Article 28 of the Confession is speaking of the visible church institute. It is the church from which one can (but ought not) "withdraw himself, to live in a separate state from it." No one is able to withdraw himself, and live in separation, from the invisible church of the decree of election. The church of Article 28 is the church that believers are called willingly and actively to *join*. One does not join the company of the elect. He is put in this company by divine decree.

The church of Article 28, which all must join, has "doctrine and discipline," to which the one who joins must submit. "Doctrine and discipline" are the offices and order of the church institute.

The church of Article 28 is a "congregation [that]…God hath established" all over the world. God establishes the church institute. This is what "institute" means: established.[2]

According to Article 29 of the Belgic Confession, this church—the church of Article 28—that all must join has marks identifying it to believers, so that they know with certainty that they are joining a true church of Christ. Marks inhere in and belong to the institute.

Beyond any shadow of doubt, Article 28 of the Belgic Confession refers to the visible church institute. This is the church that every believer is bound to join. Outside this church is no salvation.

All the Reformation Creeds Opposed to Reed

In its doctrine of the church, the Belgic Confession is in harmony with all the other Reformed creeds. Also the second aspect of Reed's tactic regarding Article 28 of the Belgic Confession is false, that is,

2. Ibid.

Reed's charge that the Belgic Confession contradicts the other Reformation creeds (15).

The Heidelberg Catechism teaches in several places that all must join and remain faithful members of a true institute, because out of it is no salvation. The Catechism teaches the necessity of church membership in Question and Answer 65:

> Since, then, we are made partakers of Christ and all his benefits by faith only, whence cometh this faith?
> The Holy Ghost works it in our hearts by the preaching of the holy Gospel, and confirms it by the use of the holy Sacraments.[3]

The working and confirming of faith, by which faith one has Christ and his benefits, is salvation. Salvation is enjoyed where there is the preaching of the gospel and the administration of the sacraments, that is, within the church institute. The Catechism gives no assurance that the Spirit works faith and thus bestows salvation otherwise.

Especially powerful is Question and Answer 83 of the Catechism. Here the Catechism teaches that the "kingdom of heaven is opened to believers" by "the preaching of the holy Gospel and Church discipline."[4] The opening of the kingdom of heaven to one is the salvation of the elect believer his life long. This salvation he enjoys, and can only enjoy, as a member of the church institute, which possesses and exercises the "office of the keys."

Also the Catechism's explanation of the fourth commandment, concerning Sabbath observance, implies that Christ saves his people within the church institute. Diligent attendance at church is required for learning the word of God and using the sacraments. The word

3. Heidelberg Catechism, Q&A 65, in ibid., 3:328.
4. Heidelberg Catechism, Q&A 83, in ibid., 3:337.

and sacraments are the means by which the Spirit saves believers and their children. These means are found in the church institute.

In addition, the Catechism declares that this diligent attendance at church is a requirement of the fourth commandment.[5] One who refuses, or neglects, to attend church—the church that preaches and administers the sacraments, that is, the church institute—is living in disobedience to the fourth commandment. No one living impenitently in disobedience to one of God's commandments—and a commandment belonging to the first table at that—can consider himself saved. Often, Protestant Reformed consistories discipline members for despising the means of grace, that is, refusing to attend church as God commands in the fourth commandment.

Article 28 of the Belgic Confession is in harmony with the French Confession of Faith (1559). The French Confession teaches the duty of every Reformed believer to be a member of the church institute.

> Now as we enjoy Christ only through the gospel, we believe that the order of the Church, established by his authority, ought to be sacred and inviolable, and that, therefore, the Church can not exist without pastors for instruction, *whom we should respect and reverently listen to, when they are properly called and exercise their office faithfully*. Not that God is bound to such aid and subordinate means, but because *it pleaseth him to govern us by such restraints*.[6]

Calvin's thumbprint is all over this article, particularly the phrase "the order of the Church." The phrase makes plain that the reference is to the church institute.

---

5. See the Heidelberg Catechism, Q&A 103, in ibid., 3:345.

6. French Confession of Faith, Article 25, in *Reformed Confessions of the 16th Century*, ed. Arthur C. Cochrane (Philadelphia: Westminster Press, 1966), 153; emphasis added.

Article 26 of the French Confession of Faith warns against remaining separate from the church institute.

> We believe that no one ought to seclude himself and be contented to be alone; but that all jointly should keep and maintain the union of the Church, and submit to the public teaching, and to the yoke of Jesus Christ, wherever God shall have established a true order of the Church.

And then this: "For if they do not take part in it [that is, the church institute], or if they separate themselves from it, they do contrary to the Word of God."[7]

Lest anyone still argue that the reference is to the invisible church of election, I note that Article 27 of the French Confession declares that this church, which no one may "seclude himself" from, has distinguishing marks that identify it and also that there may be "hypocrites and reprobates" in it.

Ominous for all those who are content to live apart from the office of the ministry of the gospel and sacraments, as do the practitioners of the house church ecclesiology, is this condemnation by all Reformed believers who share the doctrine of the church of the French Confession of Faith: "We detest all visionaries who would like, so far as lies in their power, to destroy the ministry and preaching of the Word and sacraments."[8]

In its time, the Second Helvetic [Swiss] Confession (1566) was "the most widely received among Reformed Confessions."[9] "It re-

---

7. French Confession of Faith, Article 26, in ibid.

8. French Confession of Faith, Article 25, in ibid., 153.

9. Arthur C. Cochrane, "Introduction" to the Second Helvetic Confession, in ibid., 220.

mains the official statement in most of the Reformed Churches of Eastern Europe and the Hungarian Reformed Church in America."[10] Its author was Heinrich Bullinger, the reformer of Zurich.

Immediately following its treatment of the government and "notes or signs of the true church," and therefore, referring to the church institute, the Second Helvetic says this concerning the necessity of being a member of the church.

> *Outside the Church of God There Is No Salvation.* But we esteem fellowship with the true Church of Christ so highly that we deny that those can live before God who do not stand in fellowship with the true Church of God, but separate themselves from it. For as there was no salvation outside Noah's ark when the world perished in the flood; so we believe that there is no certain salvation outside Christ, who offers himself to be enjoyed by the elect in the Church; and hence we teach that those who wish to live ought not to be separated from the true Church of Christ.[11]

10. Ibid., 221.

11. Second Helvetic Confession, Chapter 17, in ibid., 266. In the next paragraph, the Second Helvetic recognizes that its statement concerning salvation only in the church is the rule, and that there are exceptions, for example, persons who are "forced by necessity" to abstain from the sacraments. Also the Westminster Confession allows for exceptions to the rule that there is no salvation outside the church institute: "out of which there is no ordinary possibility of salvation" (Westminster Confession of Faith, 25.2, in Schaff, Creeds of Christendom, 3:657; emphasis added). Although the Belgic Confession does not express that there can be exceptions to the rule that there is no salvation outside the church institute, this must be understood concerning the statement of the rule by the Belgic Confession. For example, covenant children who die before

With reference to the instituted congregation, from which it is possible that some "separate themselves," the Second Helvetic Confession declares, "Outside the Church of God There Is No Salvation."

The paragraph of the Second Helvetic just quoted gives the lie also to another charge that Kevin Reed makes against *Bound to Join*. He takes it ill of me that I compare membership in the church institute to the salvation of Noah and his family in the ark.

> Professor Engelsma takes up the ark analogy on page 4 of his book and applies it to "the instituted church." Now, we trust that Professor Engelsma does not believe in apostolic succession. Nevertheless, his designation of the ark as a representation of the church institute smacks of a Cyprianic error, in contrast to general Reformed ecclesiology which speaks in *absolute* terms only of the invisible, universal church (14).

---

baptism are not members of the institute, but are not lost. In light of Westminster's and the Second Helvetic's recognition of exceptions to the rule and in view of the overall teaching of the Belgic Confession, *Bound to Join* notes that the rule in Article 28 of the Belgic Confession should be understood as allowing for exceptions (*Bound to Join*, 5). With typical eagerness to find fault, Reed is quick to charge the author of *Bound to Join* (not Westminster or the Second Helvetic) with "inconsistency" (14). Exceptions to a rule are not evidence of inconsistencies. As the proverb has it, "Exceptions establish the rule." Exceptions must not be appealed to in order to weaken a rule, nor become a club with which to bludgeon the rule to death, much less become the rule. The Second Helvetic Confession has more to say on the necessity of church membership in Chapter 22, including the warning that "as many as spurn such meetings [of the church institute] and stay away from them, despise true religion" (Second Helvetic Confession, Chapter 22, in *Reformed Confessions of the 16th Century, 289*).

The Second Helvetic, which not only expresses "general Reformed ecclesiology" but is also a specific Reformed confession, compares membership in the church institute to the salvation of the Old Testament church in the ark.

Calvin did the same. Commenting on Genesis 7:17, Calvin wrote: "In the same manner, the Church is fitly, and justly, compared to the ark."[12] The reference is to the church institute. Calvin has just written, "It is necessary for us to separate ourselves from the greater multitude, that the Lord may snatch us from destruction." He immediately added, "*In the same manner*, the Church is...compared to the ark." Separation from the wicked world, to escape destruction, does not apply to the universal body of the elect but to the church institute. Calvin went on to say that the spiritual ark—the church—he had in mind is characterized by "the word [of God]."[13] This is true of the instituted church.

It is true that Cyprian taught that outside the church institute is no salvation. Augustine taught the same. But so did Calvin and the Reformed creeds, specifically, the Belgic Confession and the Second Helvetic Confession. The Reformed faith does not cut itself off from the early church. One may observe for himself how many times Calvin quoted the early church fathers, particularly Cyprian, *favorably* in Book 4 of the *Institutes*—the section on the church.

In its doctrine of the church, the Belgic Confession, which is characteristically a creed of the Reformed churches on the continent of Europe, is in agreement also with the Presbyterian Westminster Confession of Faith. Article 2 of Chapter 25 of Westminster says about the "visible church" that "out of [it] there is no ordinary possibility of salvation."[14]

12. John Calvin, *Commentaries on the First Book of Moses Called Genesis* (Grand Rapids, MI: Eerdmans, 1948), 1:273.

13. Ibid.

14. Westminster Confession of Faith, Chapter 25.2, in Schaff, *Creeds of Christendom*, 3:657.

Westminster is referring to the church institute. It speaks of the "visible church." It describes this church, out of which ordinarily there is no salvation, as the "house and family of God," quoting 1 Timothy 3:15, which, as we have already seen, applies to the church institute. Westminster states that there is no salvation outside the church *ordinarily*. Outside the church of the elect, whether in the decree or being gathered throughout history, there is not even the *extraordinary* possibility of salvation.

And the very next article reads, "Unto this catholic visible Church Christ hath given the ministry, oracles, and ordinances of God, for the gathering and perfecting of the saints."[15] This is the church institute.

This article—Article 2 of Chapter 25 of the Westminster Confession—also bears on the controversy over church membership raised by the Presbyterian Kevin Reed in another way. Since his own creed teaches that Christ has given the ministry, oracles, and ordinances of God to the church institute for the gathering and perfecting of the saints, that is, for our salvation, how does a Presbyterian dare to criticize one who pleads with Reformed believers to join the church, which has the means of grace and salvation, and to argue, at great length and with some passion, that in fact there is salvation outside the church, where these means are lacking?

Whatever may be the answer to this question, it has been demonstrated that Article 28 of the Belgic Confession does not contradict the other Reformed creeds, but is in harmony with them. Thus, it is also demonstrated that *Bound to Join* does not neglect the collective teaching of the Reformation creeds.

The Offices

The doctrine of the church of the Reformed creeds, influenced

15. Westminster Confession of Faith, Chapter 25.3, in ibid., 3:658.

heavily by John Calvin, who rightly explained the ecclesiology of the Bible, is that the universal body and bride of Christ consisting of the elect takes form in history in true, visible institutes, organized in the offices of pastor, elder, and deacon. Each true institute is a church of Christ. Each of these institutes is *the* church of Christ in a genuine manifestation. In these institutes is Christ Jesus, the head and husband of the church, by his word and Spirit. He is present in the church saving his people by the preaching of the gospel, by the administration of the sacraments, and by church discipline, *which are offices of Christ in the church.*

The believer is bound to join the church institute, because in the church institute is salvation.

The believer is bound to join the church institute, because in the church institute is Christ.

To expect to find Christ outside the church is to expect to find a head apart from its body, or a husband apart from his bride.

To expect to find and enjoy salvation outside the church is to expect to find salvation apart from Christ.

Kevin Reed concocts a doctrine of the church of his own imagination, apart from and in opposition to the Reformed confessions, which express the teaching of the Bible. Reed's house church is a gathering of family and friends for the worship of God on the Lord's day that is unorganized and unordered. That is, it is a gathering for the worship of God that is not ordered by Christ in and by the three special offices of pastor, elder, and deacon. This gathering is devoid of the preaching of the gospel and the administration of the sacraments *by the office of pastor and teacher in the gathering*; devoid of the government of the gathering *by the office of elder in the gathering*; and devoid of the ministry of the mercy of Christ *by the office of deacon in the gathering.*

It lacks the offices of Christ.

It is, therefore, no church.

Claiming the honorable name of house *church* is another seman-
tic game that people are playing today, in this case disregarding the
creedal rules, to the confusion and even the spiritual destruction of
many.

The creeds determine what the visible church in the world is.

Informal or even formal gatherings of a religious nature on
Sunday do not constitute a church. That wandering preachers stop
in every so often to preach a sermon, and probably encourage the
group in their lawless ways, does not make a church. That the visit-
ing preacher may even administer what appear to be the sacraments,
apart from the office of the elder in the group, does not make the
group a church. That the members of the group help each other with
money and goods in their need, apart from the office of the deacon
in the group, does not make a church.

What makes a church is the *offices of Christ* in an assembly of
believers and their children.

This is why Calvin repeatedly spoke of the "order" of the church to
the Nicodemites. He defined the church in terms of the offices: "The
Holy Spirit calls all assemblies 'church' where the word is preached,
his name is purely declared, and the sacraments are administered."[16]

This is why, immediately following its teachings in Articles 28
and 29 concerning the necessity of joining the church and concerning the marks of a true church, the Belgic Confession, in Article
30, says about the church that it "must be governed by the spiritual
policy which our Lord has taught us in his Word," namely, that there
are pastors, elders, and deacons.[17]

And this is why, when the Heidelberg Catechism comes to the
all-important issue of the opening and shutting of the kingdom of

16. Calvin, *Come Out from Among Them*, 260–61.

17. Belgic Confession, Article 30, in Schaff, *Creeds of Christendom*,
3:421–22.

heaven by the preaching of the gospel and church discipline *in the church institute*—the issue of salvation—it asks the question, according to the German original: "What is the *Office* of the Keys?"[18] Everything depends on the offices, because the offices are the authoritative, effective presence of Christ himself in his body and bride.

So important is this matter of the offices in the church, not only regarding the controversy between Kevin Reed and *Bound to Join*, but also regarding what I now sense as a threat to the Reformed doctrine and practice of the church from a growing house church movement, that I judge the following long quotation of Calvin on the subject of church offices to be warranted.

> Paul shows by these words [Ephesians 4:8, 10–16] that this human ministry which God uses to govern the church is the chief sinew by which believers are held together in one body. He then also shows that the church can be kept intact only if it be upheld by the safeguards in which it pleased the Lord to place its salvation. "Christ ascended on high," Paul says, "that he might fill all things." [Eph. 4:10.] This is the manner of fulfillment: through the ministers to whom he has entrusted this office and has conferred the grace to carry it out, he dispenses and distributes his gifts to the church; and he shows himself

18. Heidelberg Catechism, Q&A 83, in ibid., 3:337. The German is "*Was ist das Amt der Schlussel?*" The translation in the *Psalter* used by the Protestant Reformed Churches does not do justice to the German original and to the fundamental truth about the church, by whose exercise of the office of preaching and discipline Christ is pleased to save his people. See *The Psalter with Doctrinal Standards, Liturgy, Church Order, and added Chorale Section*, reprinted and revised edition of the 1912 United Presbyterian *Psalter*, 13th printing (Grand Rapids, MI: Eerdmans, 1988), 16 in the section of "Doctrinal Standards, Liturgy, and Church Order."

as though present by manifesting the power of his Spirit in this his institution, that it be not vain or idle. Thus the renewal of the saints is accomplished; thus the body of Christ is built up [Eph. 4:12]; thus "we grow up in every way into him who is the Head" [Eph. 4:15] and grow together among ourselves; thus are we all brought into the unity of Christ, if prophecy flourishes among us, if we receive the apostles, if we do not refuse the doctrine administered to us. Whoever, therefore, either is trying to abolish this order of which we speak and this kind of government, or discounts it as not necessary, is striving for the undoing or rather the ruin and destruction of the church. For neither the light and heat of the sun, nor food and drink, are so necessary to nourish and sustain the present life as the apostolic and pastoral office is necessary to preserve the church on earth.[19]

Kevin Reed creates his own rough facsimile of a church, according to his own wishes or convenience, and calls it "church," regardless that the facsimile has no offices of Christ and, therefore, is not the church.

I could as well assemble a number of people in my home, divide them into two squabbling groups, go through the motions of making civil laws and of taxing my countrymen, and call my assembly the "house Congress of the United States."

This explains many things in Reed's assault on *Bound to Join*, which contends for the church of the Reformed confessions, that is, of the Bible.

It explains his opposition to the Belgic Confession's affirmation of the duty of all to join a true institute.

19. Calvin, *Institutes*, 4.3.2, 2:1055.

It explains his criticism of the Belgic Confession's warning that outside the church institute is no salvation.

It explains his disparaging of the three marks of the true church—the preaching of the gospel, the administration of the sacraments, and the exercise of church discipline—*which are listed as the marks in all the Reformed confessions,* for a mark of his own choosing—love—*despite the fact that no Reformed confession makes love a mark of the truth church.*

It explains Reed's insistence that the reading of the Bible be given equal time and significance with the preaching of the gospel as the main means of grace and salvation, if indeed he does not intend that reading the Bible replace preaching, *regardless that all the Reformed creeds make the preaching of the gospel, not the reading of the Bible, the chief means of grace.*

Pastoral Advice

I conclude my response to Kevin Reed's criticism of *Bound to Join* with pastoral advice.

I am constrained to do so because one of Reed's severest criticisms of *Bound to Join* is that "the book is woefully deficient from a practical, pastoral perspective…Engelsma's response is to hit [people seeking pastoral guidance about what to do, when facing the tragic reality of lacking a sound church in their vicinity] over the head with a series of combative, disjointed letters harping on the duty of church membership" (17–18). I merely call attention to this splendid manifestation of the love that is the outstanding mark of Kevin Reed's house church.

In this damning charge also, Mr. Reed is mistaken. *Bound to Join* is pastoral. It was pastoral in its original form as letters to distressed people in Europe, some of whom were not members of any church and others of whom were members of, or attending, false churches, because no true church was to be found anywhere in their vicinity. It is pastoral in its published form. The book gives practical, pastoral instruction concerning the vital matter of the public worship of God and the public confession of Jesus Christ in a true, instituted church to persons needing this instruction. Originally, the book was a response *requested of the author* by these persons.

It is true that the response to the pastoral instruction by some has been vehement criticism of the instruction and of the instructor. But this does not mean that the book is not pastoral. Some of the Nicodemites in France made the very same response to the same pastoral instruction of John Calvin in the writings that make up *Come Out from Among Them*. The angry response to Calvin became personal. He had to admonish some of his correspondents not to react to his instruction with caustic attacks on his person.

> It grieves me therefore, that these poor people insist so on fighting with me, that they think it is just a question of dealing with a man. They do not consider that they are up against God. I therefore beseech and admonish them to stop deceiving themselves by choosing me for their accuser.[20]

A good pastor, who can answer for souls to Jesus Christ in the judgment, is not the man who tells his audience what they like to hear, what makes them feel good about themselves and their situation, and what has the effect of making the often highly regarded "pastor" a popular man. Such a man is no pastor sent by Jesus Christ. It will go hard for him in the great day. As there are false prophets, so are there false pastors.

> They are one and the same. Beware of them!
> A good pastor tells the truth. He tells it in love for those to whom

20. Calvin, *Come Out from Among Them*, 102.

he speaks, but he tells the truth. He tells the truth even though the belief, confession, and practice of the truth will mean suffering; the loss of all things earthly, including family; and death for those to whom the good pastor speaks the truth. He tells the truth even though the result will be that he himself is hated and reproached. He never allows his love for those to whom he speaks the truth to adulterate, soften, or silence the truth. For the truth works their salvation. And a good pastor's love for those whom he instructs is the love of Christ, which purposes their spiritual and eternal good, often in the way of their physical and temporal suffering.

Bound to Join is pastoral. It speaks the truth that Calvin spoke to the Nicodemites. It speaks the truth of all the Reformed confessions. It speaks the truth, literally, word-for-word, of Article 28 of the Belgic Confession. It applies to the practice of all who claim to be Reformed, indeed, all who claim to be Christians, the doctrine of the church of 1 Timothy 3:15: "[The church institute, with the office of bishop and deacon, is] the house of God…the church of the living God, the pillar and ground of the truth." Be a living member of the church institute, whatever the cost! We are "bound to join"!

Although, thanks to persons like Kevin Reed, the critical response to the book gets most of the attention, there has also been positive response. There have been those who have left home, job, and country to join a true church. There are those who have been moved by *Bound to Join* to groan and sigh, night and day (in the language of Calvin), that God will open up the way for them to become members of a true church. And there are men and women, both in Europe and in North America, who are more thankful for the membership of themselves and their children in true churches of Christ than they were before they read the book and who are more determined than ever before to remain members of these churches.

My pastoral advice to Kevin Reed is that he repent of his false doctrine of the church, which leads professing Christians to the wicked way of life of living contentedly outside the church institute.

He is a Presbyterian. Let him, therefore, read again carefully Chapters 25–31 of his own Westminster Confession; Articles 27–35 of the Belgic Confession; and Book 4 of Calvin's *Institutes*, to learn (by the Spirit's guidance of him into the truth) that the church of God in the world is the church institute with the three marks of preaching, sacraments, and discipline.

If he himself and his family are practicing the doctrine of the house church, let him forthwith repent of his sin of despising the preaching of the gospel, the sacraments, and church discipline, that is, despising the church of Christ in her visible manifestation, and seek membership in this church wherever God has established it.

I do not refer to participation in a group of believers and their children that is the object of missions, conducted by an instituted church. Such a group has the office of the preaching of the gospel in the office of the missionary and is working toward institution. Upon such groups, I only pray God's blessing.

But I refer to the practice of house church. Such a group is not the object of missions. Such a group does not have the offices. Such a group has probably been gathering for private worship for years. Such a group sees no possibility of organization for many years in the future, if ever. The members of such a group are content with their situation, defending themselves against the admonitions of *Come Out from Among Them*, of *Bound to Join*, and of Article 28 of the Belgic Confession exactly as does Kevin Reed in his "review, with commentary," that is, in reality, his all-out attack on Reformed ecclesiology.

The Regulative Principle

If Mr. Reed finds himself in this deplorable and condemnable church situation, one of the reasons, if not the main reason, is his extreme and mistaken application of the "regulative principle of worship." The regulative principle of worship is that aspect of the second commandment of God's law that requires that the church not "worship [God] in any other way than he has commanded in his Word."[21] Whereas this principle applies to the main elements of public worship—preaching, sacraments, public prayers, and giving of alms—Reed applies the principle to every aspect of public worship, including the mere circumstances of worship. This leads Mr. Reed to conclude that a church that uses organ accompaniment, even though it sings the Psalms; a church that uses form prayers, for example, at the administration of the Lord's supper, even though the prayers are biblical; and a church that holds a special worship service in observance of Christmas, even though the service consists of only the biblical elements that characterize the other services—such a church is breaking the second commandment of the law of God. Such a church is apostate, if not false.

Holding such an extremist and mistaken view, Reed cannot possibly be a member of a congregation or denomination that practices such enormities.

I mention "denomination" because it is also Reformed and biblical that a local congregation belong to a denomination of true churches. This is another aspect of the sound, Reformed doctrine of the church that independent spirits like Kevin Reed make light of. Reed raises the subject of denominations only to disparage and criticize them (16–17). But in the long run, and often in the short run, the "perils of independency" destroy the independent congregation and, thus, deprive the saints of the means of grace and salvation.

Reed's extremist view of the application of the regulative prin-

---

21. Heidelberg Catechism, Q&A 96, in Schaff, *Creeds of Christendom*, 3:343.

ciple of worship explains in large part why he cannot join the Protestant Reformed Churches.

The question naturally arises in the mind of every Protestant Reformed reader of Mr. Reed's "review, with commentary" on *Bound to Join*, "Why does he not move a little distance from Texas to Redlands, California, or to Loveland, Colorado, to join a Protestant Reformed congregation? Why does he not ask the Protestant Reformed Churches for a missionary to work with him and his group?"

Reed answers this question in his criticism of *Bound to Join*.

He acknowledges, grudgingly, to be sure, that the Protestant Reformed Churches preach and confess the gospel of sovereign grace: "The Gospel is an exclusive message of sovereign grace. (This is one principle where Engelsma is generally correct)" (18).

Proclaiming the gospel of grace is the mark of the true church, the *chief* mark of the true church, which every human is bound to join.

But Reed could never affiliate with the Protestant Reformed Churches, because of his extremist doctrine of the regulative principle of worship.

> Contemporary churches (including some professing to be Reformed) use elaborate liturgies and ceremonies, sanction crucifixes and "pictures of Jesus," and employ a variety of man-made "aids" to worship. Services may be led by ministers sporting clerical collars and other priestly attire. Other congregations [read Protestant Reformed Churches] are content to display plain crosses or additional Romish symbols at church buildings, retain Romish festival days [that is, Christmas] or holy-days, include musical instruments in worship, and permit the singing of uninspired songs in worship (12).

This is not the first, or most ferocious, attack that Kevin Reed has launched against the Protestant Reformed Churches because of their alleged transgression of the second commandment. In 1995, Reed's Presbyterian Heritage Publications published what has to be one of the most violent denunciations of the Protestant Reformed Churches, as of every Reformed church that allows itself to be governed by Article 67 of the Church Order of Dordt, ever written. Article 67 of the Church Order of Dordt reads: "The churches shall observe, in addition to the Sunday, also Christmas."[22]

Reed's publication was titled "Christmas-Keeping and the Reformed Faith."[23]

No epithet was too strong, no charge too vehement, no iniquity too monstrous, to be laid to the account of the Protestant Reformed Churches for celebrating the birth of Jesus on December 25 each year by a special service of worship—at which the gospel is preached purely; the Psalms and spiritual songs are sung devoutly; God-glorifying public prayers are raised from the worshiping congregation; and believers and their children worship God in spirit and in truth.

Churches that observe Christmas in accordance with the Church Order of Dordt and by implication the Synod of Dordt, which made the rule, are guilty of "a monstrous renewal of the doctrines of popery and Phariseeism." Their sin is that by which the "man of sin first

22. Church Order of the Protestant Reformed Churches [adopted by the Synod of Dordt in 1618–19], Article 67, in *The Confessions and the Church Order of the Protestant Reformed Churches* (Grandville, MI: Protestant Reformed Churches in America, 2005), 399.

23. David W. Cason, "Christmas-Keeping and the Reformed Faith: A Response to Professor David J. Engelsma" (Dallas, TX: Presbyterian Heritage Publications, 1995).

began and then strengthened his dominion over the lives and consciences of men."[24]

In observing Christmas these churches come under the condemnation of 2 Kings 17:15. This text accuses Israel of rejecting God's statutes and covenant, following after idols, and going after the heathen.[25]

Article 67 of the Church Order of Dordt causes Reformed people to turn again "to the weak and beggarly elements," against which Galatians 4:9–11 warns.[26]

In that Reed's publication quotes 1 Kings 18:26 (the description of the idolatry of the Baal prophets on Mt. Carmel) as the subhead of its first chapter "The Defense of Christmas," the booklet implies, and intends to imply, that the sober Reformed Christians who worship God in a special Christmas service, specifically, the members of the Protestant Reformed Churches, are guilty of the sin of idolatry. Even the charge of image worship is too weak for Reed and his author. The charge must be idolatry.

This is not the place for explanation of the regulative principle of worship in defense of Dordt's rule and of the Protestant Reformed Churches' practice. I have written such an explanation in the book *Reformed Worship*.[27]

Suffice it to state here that the regulative principle of worship

24. Ibid., 20.
25. Ibid., 41–46.
26. Ibid., 57–61.
27. David J. Engelsma, "The Regulative Principle of Worship," "The Basis of the Regulative Principle of Worship," "The Regulative Principle of Worship Applied," and "The Regulative Principle of Worship and Singing," in David J. Engelsma, Barry Gritters, and Charles Terpstra, *Reformed Worship* (Grandville, MI: Reformed Free Publishing Association, 2004), 1–27.

applies to the elements of worship, the main worship practices, not to every circumstance of worship. Regarding the circumstances the church has liberty. The church has liberty also with regard to special services. She *must* worship on the Lord's day. She *may* worship on other days, including a day she sets aside for a special remembrance of God's gift of his Son.

The fathers of the Synod of Dordt, which was not a gathering of theologians who were ignorant of or opposed to the regulative principle, much less an assembly of Baal prophets, judged observance of Christmas to be permissible, indeed, beneficial.

The Second Helvetic Confession explicitly approved the observance of Christmas.

> *The Festivals of Christ and the Saints.* Moreover, if in Christian liberty the churches religiously celebrate the memory of the Lord's nativity, circumcision, passion, resurrection, and of his ascension into heaven, and the sending of the Holy Spirit upon his disciples, we approve of it highly.[28]

By his extremist application of the regulative principle of worship, Mr. Reed cuts himself off from true, instituted churches in the United States—churches that he himself acknowledges display the chief mark of the true church.

Doing so, he flouts the rule of Article 28 of the Belgic Confession, which is the doctrine of the church of all the Reformed confessions and the will of Christ: "bound to join."

One day, Mr. Kevin Reed will give account to Jesus Christ for himself, his family, and all others who, under his influence, substi-

---

28. Second Helvetic Confession, Chapter 24, in *Reformed Confessions of the 16th Century*, 291–92.

tuted Reed's house church for the church of Jesus Christ: "Lord, we rejected church institutes that preached the gospel of sovereign grace, administered the sacraments rightly, and exercised church discipline, because they held a worship service in observance of thy birth."

To Mr. Kevin Reed and the members of his house church, I urge the pastoral, practical warning of Article 28 of the Belgic Confession: "Out of it [the church institute] there is no salvation."

CHAPTER FOUR

༼ ᓂᓃ ༽

Postscript: Promotion of Reed's Criticism by EPC of Australia Minister Rev. C. Connors

O F ALL the criticism of *Bound to Join*, the most surprising, and disturbing, comes out of the Evangelical Presbyterian Church of Australia (EPCA).

The EPCA is an orthodox Presbyterian denomination, valiantly contending for the truth of sovereign grace in Australia.

As a Presbyterian denomination, adhering faithfully to the Westminster Standards, the EPCA would be expected vigorously to defend the offices, institution, and order of the church. Historically, the Presbyterians have been zealous for the order of the church of Christ.

Chapter 25 of the creed of the EPCA, the Westminster Confession of Faith, expresses the same high regard for the church institute as does the Reformed Belgic Confession in Articles 27–35.

Article 3 of Chapter 25 teaches that for the "gathering and perfecting of the saints, in this life," "Christ hath given the ministry, oracles, and ordinances" to the visible church. It goes on to declare that the significance of the ministry, oracles, and ordinances is nothing less than this, that Christ "doth by his own presence and Spirit, according to his promise, make them effectual" unto the salvation of the saints.[1]

---

1. Westminster Confession of Faith, Chapter 25.3, in Schaff, *Creeds of Christendom*, 3:658.

This is clear, strong insistence on the necessity of the institute and clear, strong affirmation of salvation in the institute. The article also clearly implies that men look in vain for the gathering and perfecting of the saints outside the institute with the ministry, oracles, and ordinances. Christ has promised to be present to his people in the ministry, oracles, and ordinances, making them effectual means unto salvation. He has not promised to be present, and to save, apart from them.

What Article 3 of Chapter 25 of the Westminster Confession implies, Article 2 states explicitly: "out of which there is no ordinary possibility of salvation."[2] As was observed in the response to Kevin Reed in the previous chapter, the mention in the article of the "visible Church," the statement immediately following in the next article that "unto this catholic visible Church Christ hath given the ministry, oracles, and ordinances of God," and the fact that the article speaks of no "*ordinary*" possibility of salvation make plain that the reference is to the visible, instituted church.

This is the same doctrine as that expressed in Article 28 of the Belgic Confession, in the same words: Outside the visible, instituted church of Christ is no salvation.

No one would suppose that there would be not only strong support, but also active promotion in the EPCA of the assault by Kevin Reed on the church institute and of Reed's advocacy of the house church.

Nevertheless, this is the case.

Writing in the July 2011 issue of the *Evangelical Presbyterian*, the official magazine of the EPCA, the editor of the magazine and a leading minister in that denomination, the Rev. C. Connors, comes out in support of the criticism of *Bound to Join* by Kevin Reed, adding blistering criticisms of his own. So strong is his support that he publishes, in its long entirety, Kevin Reed's twenty-one-page broadside against the book. This "review, with commentary" is, as I have shown in the previous chapters, an all-out attack

2. Westminster Confession of Faith, Chapter 25.2, in ibid., 3:657.

on the doctrine of the church in *Bound to Join* and, thus, on the doctrine of the church of the Belgic Confession, of John Calvin, and of Scripture.

By publishing Reed's criticism of *Bound to Join* as a necessary, and welcome, "caution" against the book and by recommending Reed's critical essay in opposition to a favorable review of *Bound to Join* by one of Rev. Connors' colleagues, Rev. Connors promotes the doctrine and practice of the house church of Kevin Reed. He promotes Reed's attack on the church in the EPCA and as widely as the *Evangelical Presbyterian* circulates throughout Australia and the world.

I quote the relevant passages of Connors' "editorial comment."

> *Bound to Join*...is a strident defence of Church membership. The book will...not unite the Reformed camp...This book is...likely to set believer against believer. A rhetorical use of history and the creeds, packaged in absolutist language, tends to do that...[I] assess the book as well-intentioned but unsuccessful...We must repudiate imperious ecclesiasticism...Engelsma's book does not do that...Don't take on all that he gives...A tendency to set each point he champions within antithetical extremes turns the product into a peculiarity...sectarian extremes. So, we present two reviews of this one book. The first is a positive commendation by Rev. David Higgs; the second is a caution by Mr. Kevin Reed, which will carry over into our next magazine. Read them both and the picture will be clear enough.

Connors concludes his editorial comment by informing his readers that "the EPC of Australia has encouraged and assisted ETRF [Kevin Reed's house church] with advice and ministry over recent years."[3] ·

3. Rev. C. Connors, "Two Book Reviews," *Evangelical Presbyterian* (July 2011): 8–9.

My response to the criticism of *Bound to Join* by Rev. Connors must be very brief, for as the above quotation shows, he offers no evidence of his charges and no ground for his condemnation. There is only denunciation of the book and its doctrine of the church.

Nothing more.

Evidently, Rev. Connors makes the arguments of Kevin Reed his own.

My response to Rev. Connors, therefore, is the reasoned and grounded refutation of Kevin Reed's attack on the church institute and defense of the house church in the chapter to which this is a postscript. This response includes the defense of the instituted church of Christ and the admonition that membership in it is necessary that I give both in *Bound to Join* and in this little work. For this defense and admonition, I provide grounds from the Reformed and Presbyterian creeds, from John Calvin, and from Scripture.

I mentioned that the criticism out of the EPCA is disturbing.

The *Evangelical Presbyterian* is the denominational paper of the EPCA. The masthead states that the "magazine is published with the authorization of the Presbytery of the Evangelical Presbyterian Church of Australia." The masthead sounds the caveat that the views expressed by the writers "may not necessarily be the official views of the Evangelical Presbyterian Church of Australia." Nevertheless, the editor's criticism of the doctrine of the church of *Bound to Join* and approval of the ecclesiastical thinking and practice of Kevin Reed, in the denominational magazine, reflect on the EPCA and raise questions about its doctrine of the church.

Reed disparages the visible, instituted church of Christ, if he does not reject it altogether.

Reed defends the unorganized house church (which is no church, but only a religious gathering), devoid of the offices of Christ, lacking the regular preaching of the gospel, without the sacraments, ungoverned and undisciplined by the eldership.

Reed thinks that this convenient, manmade arrangement is justified because all the Reformed and Presbyterian denominations in North America are apostate. He specifies the Protestant Reformed Churches as among these apostate churches. The reason for the condemnation is Reed's notion that musical accompaniment of the congregation's singing of the Psalms and a church's observance of Christmas by a special worship service are transgressions of the second commandment of the law of God, that is, the gross sin of image worship.

In addition, gratuitously, he vilifies the Protestant Reformed Churches for recent synodical decisions that were intended to defend the great cause of Christian schools among their people, in keeping with the rule of Article 21 of the Church Order of Dordt. Article 21 of the Dordt Church Order, which is the church order of the Protestant Reformed Churches (binding on all members and certainly on their ministers), reads: "The consistories shall see to it that there are good Christian schools in which the parents have their children instructed according to the demands of the covenant."[4]

About these decisions of the synod of the Protestant Reformed Churches, Reed writes: "Recently, Professor Engelsma's own denomination imposed restrictions on office-bearers regarding the home-schooling of their children—an action that exhibits entirely wrong notions about ecclesiastical authority." Reed passes judgment on these decisions: "an ominous abuse of church power, borrowing a characteristic of the false church that 'ascribes more power and authority to herself and her ordinances than to the Word of God' (Belgic Confession, art. 32)."[5]

Reed's judgment upon the Protestant Reformed Churches is cruel and unjust. It is a slander of true churches of Jesus Christ.

---

4. Church Order of the Protestant Reformed Churches, Article 21, in *Confessions and Church Order*, 387.

5. Reed, "Church Membership in an Age of Idolatry and Confusion," 12.

The editor of the denominational paper of the EPCA publishes all this.

He recommends all this.

He utters not one word of "caution" concerning any of Reed's pronouncements.

It is a relief and an encouragement, concerning the doctrine of the church of the EPCA, that the same issue of the magazine contains a long review of *Bound to Join* by another minister in the denomination, the Rev. David Higgs. This review commends *Bound to Join* for its defense of what is nothing other than the historic, creedal, biblical, Reformed and Presbyterian view of the church and membership in it.

> At last! a book with a high view of the Church; a high view that faithfully reflects the teaching of Scripture and the creeds; a high view that, sadly, is missing in the thinking of most who profess faith in Christ; a high view that, even more sadly, is rejected by many who claim to be Reformed...I cannot recommend *Bound to Join* highly enough.[6]

6. Rev. David Higgs, "[Review of] *Bound to Join: Letters on Church Membership,*" *Evangelical Presbyterian* (July 2011): 9–12.

CHAPTER FIVE

ᏣᎧ

Attack of the "Red Beetle"

I HAVE AN aversion to consulting the Internet for theological discussion.

The reason is that I agree with the definition of the Internet by the late columnist of the *Chicago Tribune* Mike Royko: "an electronic asylum filled with babbling loonies."

It does nothing to change my opinion that a critic on the Internet of *Bound to Join* identifies himself as the "Red Beetle."

Nevertheless, I respond to the Red Beetle's attack upon the book. The Beetle sets himself up as the authority on Calvinism. His scathing denunciation of *Bound to Join*, although devoid of any ground that could possibly move any genuine Calvinist (a genuine Calvinist is a *creedal* Calvinist, and the Red Beetle rejects the Reformed creeds), indicates that rejection of the church institute is widespread.[1] It also betrays a common misunderstanding of Calvinism, indeed of the entire sixteenth-century Reformation of the church, from which those of a teachable disposition can learn.

The Red Beetle's criticisms of *Bound to Join* are two. By requiring membership in an instituted church, the book denies salvation by grace alone. By affirming salvation only in the instituted church, the book is Roman Catholic tyranny.

---

1. For this criticism of *Bound to Join*, see "*Sola Ecclesia* [the Church Only]: 'Bound to Join by David J. Engelsma,'" http://www.youtube.com/watch?v=L2GzvlAZR00.

Denial of Grace

The first criticism of *Bound to Join* is that it is a denial of the gospel of salvation by grace alone. Because the book teaches that there is salvation only in the church institute and that elect believers should, therefore, join a true church and never separate from it, the book denies the gospel.

The Red Beetle makes the outrageous charges that the book implies a conditional salvation; that whenever someone teaches the necessity of church membership he corrupts the gospel by mixing gospel and law; and that the admonition to join a true church is a denial of *solus Christus* (Christ alone; the Beetle likes his audience to know that he is a Latin scholar).

The first thing that all Reformed Christians will observe about this foolish charge is that it condemns not the author of *Bound to Join*, but the Belgic Confession, indeed all the Reformed creeds. It is the Belgic Confession that declares concerning the visible institute of the church that "out of it there is no salvation" and that, therefore, "no person…ought to withdraw himself, to live in a separate state from it; but that all men are in duty bound to join and unite themselves with it."[2] As I have demonstrated in the preceding chapters, *all* the Reformed creeds teach the same thing. *Bound to Join* merely confronts those who profess Calvinism with the teaching of their confessions.

The Red Beetle, therefore, arrogantly and wickedly slanders the Reformed confessions, particularly the Belgic Confession. The Belgic Confession (on behalf of the truth of which De Bres gave his life, convinced that the Confession is the gospel of grace, and that the Synod of Dordt adopted, supposing that the Belgic Confession

2. Belgic Confession, Article 28, in Schaff, *Creeds of Christendom*, 3:418.

teaches the truth of sovereign grace, for the defense of which the synod was called) is, in fact, a denial of salvation by grace alone. So also are all the Reformed creeds actually heretical documents, teaching a mixture of grace and law.

Such is the lordly pronouncement of a Red Beetle.

Refutation

The truth is that the requirement of the Belgic Confession, as of John Calvin in his anti-Nicodemite writings, that the believer join a true church in no wise compromises the gospel of salvation by grace alone. Salvation is by grace alone. This grace God bestows to his elect, believing people and their children, *by means of the preaching of the gospel and the administration of the sacraments.* The salvation that this grace constantly bestows God safeguards in his people *by church discipline.* I have in preceding chapters proved that God uses means to bestow grace and demonstrated what these means are, both from the Reformed confessions and from Scripture, and I need not repeat the creedal and biblical evidence here.

God himself, therefore, commands all his people to be members of an instituted church in which these means of grace can be used.

There is another, even more important reason that believers, who are saved by grace alone, are called to be members of the church institute. This is that the purpose of gracious salvation is the public worship of God and the public confession of the lordship of Christ by every believer and his family with the congregation of Christ.

God, therefore, commands all those whom he has saved to be members of the worshiping congregation.

The Red Beetle's argument against church membership is as senseless as if a silly little child would argue, "Since I live only by eating and drinking, I have decided no longer to live in my home with my family but out in the woods, all by myself, away from the source of eating and drinking."

The consequences for the foolish child would not be as serious as the consequences of living apart from the church institute are for the Red Beetle and his followers. The child will only die physically. The Red Beetle and his followers die eternally, for "out of it [the church institute] is no salvation."

This aspect of the comparison of the argument of the Red Beetle with a foolish child only concerns the one matter of the child's finding in the home food and drink for his life. What about all the other, compelling reasons for a child to live in his home with his parents and with his brothers and sisters—the fellowship that a child both enjoys and contributes to, cooperation in the work of the family, the oversight of the child's life by the parents, and more? I use the comparison advisedly, for the Bible compares the church institute to a house, in which every believer is required to live and is expected to be living (1 Tim. 3:15). Again, the state of the Red Beetle outside the church is far worse than that of a child outside his home, dreadful as this may be, for the church is the "house of God," according to 1 Timothy 3:15. A runaway child lives apart from his parents; outside the church the Red Beetle willfully lives apart from God in Jesus Christ.

Similarly hollow is the Red Beetle's claim to honor Jesus Christ. The charge of the Beetle is that *Bound to Join* dishonors Christ because it honors the church. The Red Beetle, on the other hand, honors Christ by despising the church.

But the church is the body and bride of Jesus Christ. One can no more honor Christ by despising the church than one can honor the head of a physical body by doing injury to the body, or than one can honor a husband by holding his wife in contempt. The Beetle falls back, as do all who despise the church institute, upon the invisible company of the elect, as though Scripture applies the truth of

Christ's being head and husband of the church exclusively to the invisible church. Therefore, I note once more that the apostle calls the church institute at Corinth "the body of Christ" and the engaged bride of Christ (1 Cor. 12:27, 2 Cor. 11:2).

Against the admonition of *Bound to Join* that membership in a true, instituted church is necessary, the Red Beetle appeals to the teaching of the apostle in Philippians that Christ alone is our salvation. Indeed, the Beetle appeals to this teaching in the letter to the Philippians in support of his position that membership in a church institute is *unnecessary*, implying that the church institute is unnecessary.

So incompetent a teacher of the word of God is this self-appointed instructor in Calvinism that he overlooks that the apostle wrote of Christ as the only and complete savior *to the local, instituted congregation at Philippi*: "Paul...to all the saints in Christ Jesus which are at Philippi, with the bishops and deacons" (Phil. 1:1).

In the very epistle to which the Beetle appeals against the church institute and membership in it, the apostle calls the instituted congregation of believers and their children, with the three special offices, "church": "No church communicated with me as concerning giving and receiving, but ye only" (Phil. 4:15).

To the local congregation, the apostle applies the glorious title of "church." This is what the congregation at Philippi was. This is what every institute that has the marks of a true church is. It is the body and bride of Christ. In it Christ dwells by his Spirit and word, working salvation by the means of grace. Out of it there is no salvation.

This single text shuts the mouth of the Red Beetle. He rejects the instituted church. The only church there is, according to him, is the invisible company of the elect—the church in the decree. But Philippians 4:15 calls the *instituted congregation of believers and their children, with the bishops and deacons*, "church."

The text also indicates that one reason, among many, for belonging to the church is that the church dispenses the mercies of Christ, by the alms collected and distributed by the office of the diaconate. Outside the church institute professing Christians refuse, or neglect, to participate in this great work of Christ.

The Cross and the Church

The Red Beetle plays Christ off against his church; the head against his body; the husband against his wife; the only savior against the means he uses to save. As part of this ridiculous (and wicked) game, the Beetle claims that he disdains the church institute because of his zeal for the cross of Christ. The demand of *Bound to Join* that all believers be members of the church institute is supposed to jeopardize the cross. The thinking of the Beetle seems to be that the contention of the Belgic Confession, and of *Bound to Join*, that salvation is to be found only within the church compromises the truth that salvation is only in the cross of Christ.

Salvation is only in the cross of Christ.

The cross of Christ is preached by the church institute and heard, savingly, in the power of the Holy Spirit in the church institute. The cross of Christ is represented in the sacraments administered by the church institute and used, savingly, in the power of the Holy Spirit, in the church institute. Or the cross is preached by the church institute on the mission field.

Christ himself proclaims his cross and dispenses the salvation of the cross in and by the church institute, which possesses the means of grace. To the church institute Christ gave the office of "pastors and teachers" for the saving of the elect (Eph. 4:11–12). To the pastor of the church institute comes the calling: "Preach the word [of the cross]" (2 Tim. 4:2), with the assurance that by preaching the cross the pastor and teacher will save himself and those who hear him (1 Tim. 4:16). So has Christ bound his cross with the preaching of it in and by the church institute and such is the efficacy of the preaching of the cross by the Holy Spirit that the apostle can say to the churches in Galatia—*churches* in Galatia, not isolated individuals in front of their computers or families meeting informally on Sunday reading their Bibles— "Jesus Christ hath been evidently set forth, crucified among you" (Gal. 3:1).

Regarding the sacraments, which are, of course, administered only by the church institute, the apostle teaches that by eating and drinking the Lord's supper believers "do shew the Lord's death till he come" (1 Cor. 11:26).

To the true believer "is signified and sealed...that [he] hast part in the one sacrifice of Christ on the cross" *by "holy Baptism,"* according to the Heidelberg Catechism.[3] Likewise, according to the Catechism (which describes Calvinism and Christianity for all genuine Calvinists), the relation among cross, church institute, and believer is that the Lord's supper, administered by the institute, signifies and seals to the believer that he "dost partake of the one sacrifice of Christ on the cross and all his benefits."[4]

The Red Beetle may not take the cross of Christ upon his lips, since he has no use for it in his head or heart. Whereas Christ magnifies his cross and bestows its benefits by the preaching of the gospel by the church institute, the Red Beetle holds the institute in contempt, and with it the cross of Christ. Whereas Christ wills that his believing people publicly show and testify to his cross by partaking of the supper as administered by the church institute, the Red Beetle rejects the church institute, and with it the cross of Christ. Whereas Christ has revealed that he gives the benefits of his cross, forgiveness and holiness of life, by means of the sacraments of baptism and the Lord's supper, administered by the church institute, the Red Bee-

3. Heidelberg Catechism, Q&A 69, in ibid., 3:329; emphasis added.
4. Heidelberg Catechism, Q&A 75, in ibid., 3:332.

tle declares membership in the instituted church unnecessary and, therefore, pronounces the cross of Christ unnecessary.

The Red Beetle charges that one who teaches that outside the church institute is no salvation corrupts the gospel. That is, according to the Beetle, every one who confesses Article 28 of the Belgic Confession and Article 2 of Chapter 25 of the Westminster Confession corrupts the gospel. The truth is that, by rejecting the church institute (which preaches the gospel, administers the gospel-sacraments, disciplines in the interests of the gospel, and is the pillar and ground of the truth of the gospel), the Red Beetle does not so much corrupt the gospel as reject it altogether.

Misrepresentation

This is enough to expose and refute the first prong of the attack upon the church by the Red Beetle, except that one misrepresentation of *Bound to Join* must be rebuked. The Beetle charges that the author of *Bound to Join* teaches, and evidently believes, that all members of the visible, instituted church are elect and saved. This absurd charge allows the Beetle to put me in bed with Peter Leithart, leading theologian of the federal vision—a prospect as abhorrent to Leithart as to me.

The Red Beetle bases this baseless charge on my statement in *Bound to Join* of the "deepest reason for the necessity of church membership": "The church is the body of Christ (1 Cor. 12:27)." I then add:

> In this body he [Christ] gives each member his grace by the preaching of the gospel and by the sacraments, as the means of the Spirit of Christ. In this body he privileges each member to honor and serve him, the head, in their relation and cooperation with all the other members (Eph. 4:15–16).[5]

5. Engelsma, *Bound to Join*, 47.

What the Red Beetle deliberately ignores is that these sentences are immediately preceded by this statement: "When Christ saves *his own elect,* he does not save them in isolation from himself and from the other members. But he unites *them* to himself by uniting them to a visible manifestation of his body (v. 13 [of 1 Corinthians 12])."[6] This statement plainly qualifies the sentences that immediately follow. "Each member" who receives grace is an elect in the visible congregation.

The Beetle's interpretation of what is said of the members of the congregation (in *Bound to Join*), ignoring that the reference is to Christ's "elect," is similar to applying Paul's statement in Ephesians 1:7 that the members of the Ephesian congregation have redemption through the blood of Christ to all the members of that congregation, ignoring that Paul has qualified his reference to the members of the congregation by mentioning the elect in Ephesians 1:4.

Elsewhere *Bound to Join* recognizes that there are hypocrites and reprobates in the church institute.[7] The book quotes Article 29 of the Belgic Confession as authoritative for the Calvinist doctrine of the church. Article 29 states that "hypocrites…are mixed in the Church with the good."[8]

Bound to Join does not share the federal vision doctrine that all members of the visible institute are elect and saved. The Protestant Reformed Churches are known the world over for teaching, with Paul in Romans 9, that some of the baptized children of godly parents are reprobate. Although these children are members of the visible congregation by baptism, they, like hypocrites in the church, are not the objects or recipients of the grace of God, which is always particular, that is, for the elect only.

But the elect children of believers, with his other elect, God gathers and saves *in the church institute.*

6. Ibid.; emphasis added.
7. See ibid., 97.
8. Ibid., 162.

It is not surprising that one who is ignorant of Calvin should also be ignorant of Protestant Reformed writers. But then he should not make ludicrous charges against them.

Since the Red Beetle raises the subject of the federal vision and its doctrine of the church, foolishly trying to besmirch the doctrine of the church of Article 28 of the Belgic Confession by identifying it with that of the federal vision, I observe that it is exactly the anti-church, individualistic theology of such as the Red Beetle that occasions and gives impetus to the doctrine of the church of the federal vision.

The men of the federal vision see the low regard, indeed contempt, for the church institute of many professing Calvinists. They notice that professing Calvinists speak highly of the invisible church of the elect while disparaging the institute, if not in order to disparage the institute. They recognize that many who loudly profess Calvinism have no understanding whatever of the purpose of the work and theology of the Geneva reformer, namely, *the reform of Christ's instituted church*.

The federal vision reacts by making the instituted church the entire reality of the church, denying the invisible body of the elect, and by describing membership itself in the institute as salvation, denying that eternal predestination governs the means of grace.

This is false (church) doctrine.

By their denial of the church institute, the Red Beetle and his ilk contribute to the false doctrine of the federal vision and its spread.

Papal

This brings me to the second prong of the attack of the Red Beetle on *Bound to Join*. The Red Beetle savages *Bound to Join* as Roman Catholic doctrine of the church. The book is reminiscent of the

Roman Catholic Church. It is papal. It advocates the ecclesiastical tyranny characteristic of Rome.

The basis in Scripture, in the Reformed confessions, and in Calvin for this charge is never stated. The reason is that there is none. On the Internet, grounds for arguments and charges are not required. Violent denunciation suffices.

But the Red Beetle does assume a ground for his charge against the doctrine of the church of *Bound to Join*, and he likes his audience to assume it with him. The ground that the Beetle assumes is this: Because Rome insists that membership in its institution is necessary for salvation, all teaching that membership in a church institute is necessary must be Roman Catholic. *Bound to Join* requires membership in a true, instituted church. Therefore, *Bound to Join* is Roman Catholic.

The ground assumed by the Red Beetle may be phrased negatively. Because Rome insists on the necessity of membership in the Roman Catholic institute, it is not necessary to be a member of any institute. Anyone who teaches the necessity of church membership in any church institute is, by virtue of this fact, Roman Catholic in his doctrine of the church.

So much for the logic of the Red Beetle!

Let us apply this logic to everyday life. Because Hitler demanded submission to his evil rule, all demands for submission to any civil government are, therefore, Hitlerian and illicit.

Let us apply this logic to other aspects of Christian doctrine. Because Rome teaches the doctrine of the Trinity and the necessity of believing it, all churches that teach the Trinity and the necessity of believing it are crypto-Roman Catholic. Indeed (such is the logic of the Beetle's brain), because Rome teaches the Trinity, all who are determined not to be Roman Catholic must deny the Trinity.

Again, and bearing now on the issue between the Red Beetle and

Bound to Join, the logic of the Beetle is that because Rome insists on submission to its ecclesiastical ruler, the pope, all who insist on the submission of believers to ecclesiastical rulers *in an instituted church* make themselves guilty of ecclesiastical tyranny and show themselves to be Roman Catholic in their thinking. Therefore, when the Holy Spirit commands all believers to "obey them that have the rule over you [in the church], and submit yourselves" (Heb. 13:17), he reveals himself as a Roman Catholic Spirit. Rome will be happy to hear it. What the Spirit should have said in Hebrews 13:17 (according to the logic of the Red Beetle) is "Since the Roman Catholic Church will tyrannically command submission to the pope, no believer needs to submit to any body of elders; all demands for submission to office-bearers in a church institute are Roman Catholic tyranny."

One is tempted to despair of the usefulness of responding to such thinking. But there are those who are influenced by such thinking about the church institute to whom God may yet reveal the truth.

First, the charge of Roman Catholic tyranny falls not so much upon *Bound to Join* as upon the Belgic Confession. It is the Belgic Confession that requires all believers to join the church institute, since "out of it there is no salvation."[9] It is the Belgic Confession that goes on to teach that it pleases Christ to govern "this true church" by "the spiritual policy" that consists of the three special offices: pastors, elders, and deacons.[10] It is the Belgic Confession that adds "Every one ought to esteem the Ministers of God's Word and the Elders of the Church very highly for their work's sake, and be at peace with them without murmuring, strife, or contention, as much as possible."[11]

According to the Red Beetle, at this point in its doctrine the Bel-

9. Belgic Confession, Article 28, in Schaff, *Creeds of Christendom,* 3:418.

10. Belgic Confession, Article 30, in ibid., 3:421–22.

11. Belgic Confession, Article 31, in ibid., 3:423.

gic Confession has completely forgotten the gospel of grace, which it has taught earlier, and its controversy with Rome, in which the author of the Belgic Confession was willing to sacrifice his life, and lapsed into Roman Catholic tyranny. And when the Synod of Dordt officially adopted the Belgic Confession, including Articles 27–35 on the church, as the creed of all Reformed believers, the synod did not perceive, as does the sharp thinking of the Red Beetle, that it was imposing Roman Catholicism on the Reformed churches.

Second, the unrighteous and unwarranted demand of Rome that all belong to its false institute does not negate the righteous and warranted demand of Scripture and the Reformed creeds that all believers belong to a true institute. The demand by King Jeroboam that all the Israelites worship the calves, improperly, at the two prescribed sites did not negate the demand of God that his people worship him, properly, at the temple in Jerusalem. The demand by the false prophetess Jezebel that the saints worship God by fornicating and eating things sacrificed to idols did not annul the demand of the Lord Jesus that the saints worship God purely *in the worship services of the church in Thyatira* (Rev. 2:18–29).

Third, there are these essential differences between Rome's doctrine of the church and the Reformed doctrine of the church. Rome demands membership in its institute, which is false; the Reformed faith demands membership in an institute that is true, as determined by the marks.

Rome demands membership in the Roman Catholic Church because in it one has communion with the bishop of Rome, the pope; the Reformed faith demands membership in a true church institute because in it the believer and his children have communion with Jesus Christ, who is present with his word and Spirit in the preaching of the gospel and in the sacraments.

Rome demands membership in the Roman Catholic institution because in it one gets salvation by union with the pope and by the automatic operation of the sacraments; the Reformed faith demands membership in a true church because in it believers and their children receive grace and salvation by the preaching of the gospel and the use of the sacraments, which the Spirit of Christ freely makes effectual to elect believers, who hear the word and use the sacraments in faith.

Rome demands membership in the Roman Catholic Church because in it one worships God and honors Christ especially by the abomination of the mass; the Reformed faith demands membership in a true church because in it believers and their children carry out their high calling of engaging in the public worship of God in the preaching and believing of the gospel, in the use of the sacraments, in the communion of the saints, and in the public prayers and songs.

In short, Rome demands membership in the Roman Catholic Church, *falsely* claiming to be the body and bride of Christ; a Reformed congregation demands membership in itself as the *genuine* body and bride of Jesus Christ.

Church Membership Demanded

Indicating a heresy that runs through his wretched doctrine of the church and likely produces it, the heresy of antinomianism, the Red Beetle asserts that the gospel never demands us to join a church or to be a member of a church.

The gospel demands church membership in Article 28 of the Belgic Confession. The demand "bound to join" is an integral part of the gospel, which the Belgic Confession sets forth in its fullness— not only the five points of Calvinism, but also the true church and membership in it.

The gospel demands church membership in Question and Answer 103 of the Heidelberg Catechism. The fourth commandment of the law, which the Catechism describes as the demand of the gospel for a thankful, holy life, requires every believer—every genuine Calvinist—diligently to attend church, to learn the word of God by hearing the preaching of the gospel, to use the sacraments, to call publicly upon the Lord with the worshiping congregation, and to give Christian alms when the deacons pass the plate. The believer does all this, and *can only* do all this, by membership in a church institute.[12]

The gospel demands church membership in its dreadful warnings against separating from the visible, instituted church. First John 2:19 warns that those who abandon the visible institute (no one can go out from the invisible body of the elect) go out from us, but are not of us.

Hebrews 10:25–31 warns against "forsaking the assembling of ourselves together, as the manner of some is." It adds the awful threat that this amounts to sinning willfully after one has received the knowledge of the truth and treading underfoot the Son of God, so that the end of one who thus despises the church institute is damnation. "It is a fearful thing to fall into the hands of the living God."

The gospel demands church membership by positive exhortations. Ephesians 4:3 calls the (Ephesian) believer to endeavor to keep the unity of the Spirit in the bond of peace (in the church at Ephesus). Hebrews 13:17 requires believers and their children to submit to the elders of the church institute.

The gospel demands church membership by the presupposition that runs throughout the entire New Testament, namely, that all elect believers and their children are placed by God in an instituted church of Christ, where they are saved by the keys of the kingdom and in which they serve the body and its head.

Most of the epistles are addressed to churches, and to individual believers as members of the churches (1 Cor. 1:2, Gal. 1:2, etc.). If

12. Heidelberg Catechism, Q&A 103, in ibid., 3:345.

an epistle is not addressed to a church, it usually indicates somewhere in the content that it has an instituted church in view. Romans is not addressed to the church, but to the saints (Rom. 1:7). Mention in chapter 12, however, of gifts of teaching and ruling shows that the saints in Rome were members of an instituted church or of instituted churches.

In Revelation 2–3, the Lord addresses the seven churches, indicating both the full reality of the church, that is, the universal body of the elect taking form in the institute, and the fact that believers are members of instituted churches, which have an "angel," that is, the office of pastor and teacher.

First Timothy 3, in addition to giving the qualifications of officebearers, teaches by implication that all believers are bound to join and remain members of the church institute. In fact, 1 Timothy 3:15 expressly *states* the necessity of membership in the church institute. The apostle instructs Timothy "how thou oughtest to behave thyself in…the church." "Oughtest" is the Authorized Version's translation of the Greek word meaning "it is necessary."

If it is necessary to *behave* in a certain way in the church, that is because it is necessary to *be* in the church, in the first place. The Holy Spirit certainly does not mean that membership in the church is optional, but that if one chooses to be a member he ought to behave in an appropriate manner. The statement that it is necessary to behave properly in the church is similar to parents admonishing their children, "It is necessary that, living in the home (as you necessarily do), you behave according to the rules of the house." The necessity of proper behavior is at bottom the deeper and even more urgent necessity of *being* in the house, of *being a member* of the household.

What Paul says to Timothy, he says to him not only as a pastor, but also as a believer. Not only officebearers, but also all the members must live in the house of God, which is the church, in the manner prescribed in 1 Timothy.

The church in view in 1 Timothy 3:15 is not the invisible, universal body of the elect. Neither is it some manmade, unorganized, and disorganized gathering of family and friends for religious activities. It is the church established by the Lord Jesus Christ in the offices of bishop and deacon, as the preceding verses in 1 Timothy 3 make plain.

First Timothy 3:15, therefore, is the inspired, authoritative, perfectly clear word of the Spirit of Christ to and concerning all believers, everywhere and always: It is necessary to live in the church institute and to do so with proper behavior.

All those today who live apart from the church institute are disobeying the explicit word of Jesus Christ in 1 Timothy 3:15. All those today who fight the necessity of membership in the church institute are fighting not a merely human book and author, but Holy Scripture and its divine author.

No Calvinist

The Red Beetle rejects the church institute. The Beetle contends that the universal, invisible company of the elect is the full and exclusive reality of the church. He denies that anyone needs to be a member of an instituted congregation.

The Red Beetle, therefore, is no Calvinist. A Calvinist is one who heeds the biblical instruction of John Calvin not only concerning certain important doctrines of salvation, but also concerning the church. He or she has read and finds biblical the teaching of Calvin not only in the first three books of the *Institutes*, about creation and redemption, but also in the fourth book, about the church.

The Red Beetle supposes he is a Calvinist, because he has the five points of Calvinism rattling around in his head, and because he likes to argue about them on the Internet. This no more makes him a Calvinist than my knowing that two plus two is four makes me a mathematician, or my knowing that husbands rule their wives makes me a husband. There is far more required of a mathematician than knowing that two plus two is four, basic as this axiomatic, mathematical truth is. There is far more required to be a husband than knowing that a husband rules, fundamental as this marital truth is. And there is far more required of a genuine Calvinist than an intellectual assent to the five points, essential as a believing understanding, embrace, and confession of these five doctrines are.

Calvin was a churchman—a churchman not only or even mainly with regard to the invisible church of election, but also and especially with regard to the church institute. To and on behalf of the church institute, he devoted all his life and work.

Like Luther, like all the reformers, indeed, like the entire six-teenth-century Reformation, Calvin's purpose was not simply the recovery of sound doctrine, much less only the recovery of the sound doctrine of the five points of Calvinism, as they are popularly called. Calvin's purpose was certainly the recovery of sound doctrine, particularly the recovery of the truth of salvation by sovereign grace. This is the gospel.

But Calvin, like the other reformers, purposed the recovery of the gospel *on behalf of a re-formed church—a re-formed church institute.* God's people, the body and bride of Christ, the church institute, must have the gospel of grace—*in the preaching of that gospel and in the sacraments, which are signs and seals of that gospel.*

This was Christ's purpose with the Reformation. The Reformation was the lover in the Song of Solomon seeking his bride.

Had Calvin been confronted by the notion that the Reformation was merely about recovering five points of doctrine, and not about a re-formed church institute, his first reaction would have been stupefied astonishment. His second would have been a tract against those peddling this notion that would have been far more severe than is this response to the Red Beetle.

In fact, there is neither effective witness to nor maintenance of the five points apart from the church institute, for the church institute is "pillar and ground of the truth," including the truth of sovereign grace (1 Tim. 3:15).

The Red Beetle is no Calvinist. A Calvinist is one who adopts, loves, confesses, and lives the Reformed creeds, which are the authoritative statement and standard of the Reformed faith. A Calvinist is not every Tom, Dick, or Harry holding forth on the Internet. The Red Beetle rejects the Reformed creeds, particularly Articles 27–35 of the Belgic Confession.

Quick as he is to charge "Roman Catholicism" against the author of *Bound to Join*, which has a visceral effect in some who do not bother to examine the evidence, the fact is that the Red Beetle is one of the best accomplices Rome has. The main attraction of Rome to Protestants is Rome's claim to be the church and, thus, to offer communion with God and his people, salvation, and comfort in life and death. Experiencing the need for the church, Protestants who are told by the Red Beetle that Calvinism has no church and no church membership will turn to Rome.

Come home to mother church is the seductive call of Rome.

Calvin did not respond by denying that there is a mother church. But he contended that the true, instituted church of the Reformation, particularly of the Reformed faith and practice, is the genuine mother church.

> Because it is now our intention to discuss the visible church, let us learn even from the simple title "mother" how useful, indeed how necessary, it is that we should know her. For there is no other way to enter into life unless this mother conceive us in her womb, give us birth, nourish us at her breast, and lastly, unless she keep us under her care and guidance until, putting off mortal flesh, we

become like the angels [Matt. 22:30]. Our weakness does
not allow us to be dismissed from her school until we
have been pupils all our lives. Furthermore, away from her
bosom one cannot hope for any forgiveness of sins or any
salvation, as Isaiah [Isa. 37:32] and Joel [Joel 2:32] testify.[13]

The Red Beetle presents himself as a Calvinist and evidently is
regarded by some as the authority on Calvinism. Others who regard themselves as Calvinists are similarly disparaging the instituted
church and denying the necessity of membership in it, as though
this rejection of the church were true to the teaching of John Calvin.
Therefore, I conclude my response to the Red Beetle by quoting Calvin at some length on the importance of the church institute and on
the necessity of membership in it. The quotation is part of Calvin's
Catechism of the Church of Geneva.

Having defined the Church as "the body and society of believers
whom God hath predestined to eternal life,"[14] Calvin then asked and
answered the following questions.

> *M[inister]. Can this Church be known in any other way than
> when she is believed by faith?*
> S[tudent, in catechism]. There is indeed also a visible
> Church of God, which he has described to us by certain
> signs and marks.
>
> *Why do you subjoin forgiveness of sins to the Church?*
> Because no man obtains it without being previously

13. Calvin, *Institutes*, 4.1.4, 2:1016.
14. John Calvin, "Catechism of the Church of Geneva," in *Calvin's
Tracts*, ed. Henry Beveridge (Edinburgh: Calvin Translation Society,
1849), 2:50.

united to the people of God, maintaining unity with the body of Christ perseveringly to the end, and thereby attesting that he is a true member of the Church.

In this way you conclude that out of the Church is nought but ruin and damnation?

Certainly. Those who make a departure from the body of Christ, and rend its unity by faction, are cut off from all hope of salvation during the time they remain in this schism, be it however short.[15]

The mention of departing from the church, of rending its unity, and of the possibility of repenting this schism makes clear that Calvin here was speaking of the church institute.

"Those who make a departure from the body of Christ…are cut off from all hope of salvation."

Thus, Calvin, on the necessity of church membership.

Thus, genuine Calvinism.

---

15. Ibid., 2:51–52.

CHAPTER SIX

ᔐᕈ

Review by a Reformed Pastor

J OHN BOUWERS, pastor in the United Reformed Churches, re-
viewed *Bound to Join* in the periodical *Christian Renewal*.[1] The
review was favorable. "The book…addresses a real need. It is
helpful in many ways." "Engelsma does a good job highlighting the
concern we ought to have for the ordinary means of grace out of rev-
erence for God and with love for the truth." "There is some interest-
ing history and some good contemporary challenges." "[The book]
provides a helpful, Christ-centered summary of the concern being
addressed in B[elgic] C[onfession] Article 29."

Especially gratifying is that the Reformed pastor grasped and ap-
preciated the urgent, spiritual, practical concern of the book. Bouwers' opening paragraph identifies this concern.

> It cannot be denied that the church of the Lord Jesus
> Christ is not esteemed as it ought to be today. It must
> certainly also be lamented that the value, even the duty of
> being joined to a true and faithful church is not appreci-
> ated and acted upon by many.[2]

1. John Bouwers, "Engelsma on Church Membership, *Bound to Join:
Letters on Church Membership*," *Christian Renewal* (June 8, 2011): 38–39.
   2. Ibid., 38.

No doubt because of his own experience as a pastor with members who leave the church or with nonmembers who refuse to join the church for unsubstantial, subjective reasons, Bouwers expressed appreciation for the book's insistence on determining church membership by the objective marks that are listed in Article 29 of the Belgic Confession.

He was well aware, as every Reformed pastor at the beginning of the twenty-first century ought to be, of the apostasy of many churches both in the Netherlands and in North America. The warning sounded in *Bound to Join*, therefore, is not resented, but approved. "We should take heed. That also means that if we belong to a faithful church we must also never let down our guard but always contend for the faith and love the truth."[3]

Bouwers' criticisms of the book are both fair and constructive. One is that the book, consisting as it does of letters, "tends to meander somewhat [and] gets a little repetitive." Another is the "nondescript chapter headings."[4]

Distinctives

The third and main criticism is "the amount of time the author spends defending Protestant Reformed distinctives." The result, according to the Rev. Bouwers, is that "some less than charitable conclusions are drawn by Engelsma with regard to the churches that allow for the positions the PRC are renowned for opposing."[5]

It is this third criticism that occasions response to the Rev. Bouwers' review of *Bound to Join*.

I do not intend to respond to the criticism that *Bound to Join* contains too much defense of the doctrines confessed and the practices followed by the Protestant Reformed Churches. Bouwers

3. Ibid., 39.
4. Ibid., 38.
5. Ibid., 39.

himself recognizes that this was not my intention with the book. I was drawn into doing so by those in Europe with whom originally I was corresponding. "From the outset he [the author of *Bound to Join*] appeared determined not to go in that direction [namely, 'defending the Protestant Reformed distinctives'], insisting that his purpose in writing the letters was not the promotion or defense of these churches."[6]

Nor will I challenge Bouwers' observation that some of my conclusions regarding churches that oppose doctrines and practices held and followed by the Protestant Reformed Churches are "less than charitable." So it seemed to that reviewer. Every reader can judge for himself. I have reexamined the conclusions in light of Bouwers' judgment.

My sole interest in responding to the review by Rev. Bouwers is his description of the doctrines and practices that separate the Protestant Reformed Churches from Bouwers' United Reformed Churches and from many other Reformed and Presbyterian churches as "Protestant Reformed distinctives."[7]

This is a serious mistake. By no means is this a mistake only or mainly on the part of Rev. Bouwers.

It is a mistake made by many other Reformed and Presbyterian theologians and ministers.

It is a mistake that is found occasionally in the Protestant Reformed Churches.

My intention in correcting this mistake is not at all to criticize the reviewer of *Bound to Join*. Rather, I do what I can to correct the mistake in the Reformed community of churches. Also, I am concerned that the Protestant Reformed Churches themselves not fall into the error, namely, viewing the doctrines and practices that separate them from other Reformed churches as mere "distinctives."

6. Ibid., 39.
7. Ibid., 39.

Although Rev. Bouwers does not identify the doctrines and practices of the Protestant Reformed Churches to which he refers, in light of his statement that they are doctrines and practices for which these churches are "renowned" and in light of the fact that they are the doctrines and practices mentioned in *Bound to Join*, there can be no doubt what they are.

They are the doctrine of particular, sovereign grace in the preaching of the gospel, as opposed to the well-meant offer; the doctrine of the antithesis, as opposed to the doctrine of common grace; and the doctrine of an unconditional covenant of grace, governed by eternal election, in opposition to the doctrine of a gracious but conditional covenant established with all the baptized babies of believers alike.

Rev. Bouwers refers to the doctrine and practice of the lifelong bond of marriage between one man and one woman, as the symbol of God's faithful, unbreakable covenant with his people in Jesus Christ. He has in mind the Protestant Reformed teaching, with its practice among the membership of the churches, that the fifth commandment of the law of God (to say nothing of the sixth, which forbids ungodly violence, indeed murder) forbids membership in worldly labor unions.

It is not my purpose to argue these issues.

Rev. Bouwers is a knowledgeable former minister in the Christian Reformed Church and a present minister in the United Reformed Churches. He knows the issues. I have no doubt that he has considered the grounds put forward by the Protestant Reformed Churches on behalf of all these doctrines and practices.

Besides, it is not the purpose of this work to enter into such theological debates. This book responds to criticism of *Bound to Join* on behalf of the right doctrine and practice of the church—ecclesiology.

In *Bound to Join*, the doctrines and practices that Bouwers describes as "Protestant Reformed distinctives" were brought up as belonging to the marks of the true church, which all Reformed believers should join, according to Articles 28 and 29 of the Belgic Confession.

Viewing these doctrines and practices as mere distinctives challenges the significance that *Bound to Join* attributed to them.

In the parlance of conservative Reformed and Presbyterian theologians, ministers, and even church members, the distinctives of the various churches are those teachings and practices that, although important to the denomination and although setting a denomination off from others, are not essential to the Reformed faith and life. When ministers speak of the distinctives of the various Reformed denominations, their thinking is that all the denominations share the fundamental doctrines of the Reformed faith, as summarized by the creeds, and have in common the fundamentals of the Reformed, Christian life. But all denominations in addition have their distinctives, which, if they are not mere quirks and oddities, nevertheless do not touch the fundamentals of the faith and life.

A church's distinctives in the sphere of Reformed Christianity are what Article 85 of the Church Order of Dordt calls "nonessentials."[8]

There are such distinctives, such nonessentials, among us.

Aware that with regard to some of the teachings and practices that I will mention, the churches that are distinguished by them hold that they are, in fact, fundamental, and with no intention of offending any, I make bold to mention by way of illustration what *I* consider to be such distinctives.

Whether a church sings the Psalms with or without musical accompaniment is, in my opinion, a nonessential, a mere distinctive.

Leaving aside for the moment the requirement of Article 67 of the Church Order of Dordt, a church's observance of Christmas by a special worship service is a distinctive.

8. Church Order of the Protestant Reformed Churches, Article 85, in *Confessions and Church Order*, 403.

Requiring the female members to wear head-coverings is, in my judgment, a distinctive.

Teaching predestination as infralapsarian, rather than as supralapsarian, is a nonessential.

If full justice is done to the immediate regeneration of elect infants in their infancy, and if the teaching of mediate regeneration does not compromise the sovereignty and irresistibility of grace, teaching mediate regeneration, rather than immediate regeneration, is a nonessential.

Taking into account the necessity of baptizing infants, the mode of baptizing is a distinctive.

The importance of recognizing distinctives, or, in the words of the Church Order of Dordt, "nonessentials," the Church Order of Dordt points out in the article in which it mentions nonessentials: "Churches whose usages differ from ours merely in nonessentials shall not be rejected."[9]

The unity of the body of Christ, manifested in the organizational oneness of congregations and denominations, is of vital importance to the Reformed faith. As we love the church and her head, we are zealous for the church's unity. We mourn the divisions in her institutional form in the world. We pray and work for a fuller manifestation of her oneness.

Mere distinctives may not stand in the way, may not contribute to the divisions.

Such is the Reformed, Christian faith concerning the church.

Such is the *rule* of the Reformed church order.

Speaking for myself, I would be willing to give up musical accompaniment of congregational singing for union with other churches, if only the condition were not that I had to judge musical accompaniment violation of the second commandment.

9. Ibid.

If this would make for church unity, I would try to get all Protestant Reformed women to wear head-coverings at worship services, again on the condition that failure to wear a covering would not be considered a sin.

If the only barrier to the manifestation of the oneness of the body of Christ were observance of Christmas by a special worship service, I would regretfully give this up, unless, again, the condition of church union was judging such observance the will-worship condemned by the second commandment.

Difference regarding infralapsarianism and supralapsarianism may not cause division or prevent union, so long as I may preach that Jesus Christ is first and foremost in the eternal counsel of God—before the decree of the church, before the decree of the creation, before the decree of the fall.

I would be willing to do or give up these things because I would regard doing or giving up these things my calling from Christ. Nonessentials may not hinder unity, much less cause disunity.

The doctrines and practices of the Protestant Reformed Churches that distinguish and separate these churches from the other Reformed churches are not distinctives, are not nonessentials. They are, rather, doctrines that are fundamental to the gospel of salvation by grace alone and practices that are basic to the Christian life.

Insofar as the other Reformed churches depart from these doctrines and practices, they depart from the creedal, biblical Reformed faith and compromise the Christian life. This judgment, I suspect, is what Rev. Bouwers had in mind when, in his review, he lamented a lack of charity. But condemnation of certain doctrines and practices that have taken hold in churches is not necessarily a lack of love, unless much of the message of both the prophets and the apostles in Scripture betrays a lack of love.

That their distinguishing doctrines and practices are fundamental Reformed theology and basic Christian walk is the conviction of the Protestant Reformed Churches. For this conviction they have grounds, with which Rev. Bouwers and many others are familiar. I will not adduce them here.

But it must be inescapably evident to all that these doctrines and practices do not fall into the category of mere distinctives. They are of a different kind, of a different order, than holding or not holding a special worship service in observance of Christmas, or using or not using an organ or a piano to sing the songs of Zion in worship, or baptizing by sprinkling or by pouring. Even the charge by the Protestant Reformed Churches that deviation from the doctrines and disregard for the practices are sinful carries weight on the very face of the charge.

I demonstrate.

The Preaching as Particular Grace

The Protestant Reformed confession that the saving grace of God in the preaching of the holy gospel is particular—for the elect alone—and sovereign—so that all to whom God shows and bestows this grace are saved by this grace—is based on and in harmony with the defense of sovereign, particular grace in the Canons of Dordt, as in all the Reformed confessions. The Protestant Reformed confession of particular grace in the preaching is not something "off the wall," is not a teaching without any obvious creedal basis, is not an insight devoid of backing in the history of the Reformed churches. It certainly does not concern a relatively insignificant truth in the Reformed tradition, in the Reformed creeds, and in Scripture. It concerns (saving) grace, the preaching of the gospel, the salvation of sinners, and the glory of God in salvation.

The opposition to the doctrine of particular grace in the preaching takes the form of the teaching of the well-meant offer. The well-meant offer, *according to its proponents*, teaches that the saving grace of God in Jesus Christ in the gospel is extended by God more widely than election, is motivated by a desire of God for the salvation of all men without exception, and is resistible. The proponents of the well-meant gospel offer cannot demonstrate that this doctrine does not contradict the Canons of Dordt or differs from the Arminian heresy of universal, resistible grace.

In addition, all Reformed churches in North America are aware, or can be aware, of the development of the doctrine of the well-meant offer in the Christian Reformed Church, which adopted it as official church dogma in 1924. In the 1960s, Prof. Harold Dekker publicly advocated universal atonement *with explicit appeal to the doctrine of the well-meant offer as a basis and source of this heresy.* In the 1980s, Dr. Harry Boer criticized the doctrine of predestination as confessed by the Canons of Dordt in the first head, again with explicit appeal to the doctrine of the well-meant offer.

Today, there are not half a dozen ministers in the Christian Reformed Church who preach particular, sovereign grace, and not one who is publicly contending for sovereign grace against its foes. The Canons of Dordt are a dead letter in that denomination. The leaders are presently devising a radical change of the Formula of Subscription, mainly to free the ministers and theologians of the Canons and their doctrine of election and reprobation.

The theology of the well-meant offer, once proposed in that church as the paradoxical complement to particular, sovereign grace, has thoroughly leavened the whole lump.

The Antithesis

The Protestant Reformed Churches teach the antithesis, or spiritual separation, between the church and the world, between the Reformed believer and the world of the ungodly. The antithesis is fundamental to the life of the church, both in the Old Testament and in the New Testament, rooted as it is in the first promise of the gospel in Genesis 3:15: "I will put enmity." The great danger for Israel in the

Old Testament was friendship with the ungodly nations. The great danger for the church in the New Testament is worldliness. This is not something that only a few theologians can perceive by dint of hard study of the original manuscripts of the Bible. It lies on the surface of Scripture, plain to the rudest reader.

In its concern for the antithesis, the Protestant Reformed Churches reject the doctrine of a common grace of God.

According to its proponents and defenders, this is the teaching that church and world have a grace of God in common—*a grace of God*. Having this grace in common, the people of God and the children of the devil have a solid basis for a certain friendship. Indeed, by virtue of this grace, they can and must cooperate in the spiritual work of "Christianizing" society, a nation, the whole world.

Because the world of ungodly men and women possess the grace of God, their thinking must be respected, indeed accepted, as God's own truth, for example, the world's thinking about origins—evolution, not creation; the world's thinking about the perfect equality of men and women in all respects, resulting in the denial of the headship of the husband in marriage and in women in ecclesiastical office; and the world's thinking about sexual ethics, specifically the goodness and legitimacy of sodomy and lesbianism.

After some one hundred years of the workings of the doctrine of common grace in the Reformed Churches in the Netherlands, the Free University of Amsterdam, the Christian Reformed Church, and Calvin College (all of which committed themselves in an overt, enthusiastic way to the doctrine of common grace), it is apparent to the Protestant Reformed Churches that their founding fathers were right in warning that there is death in that pot. Common grace destroys the antithesis. Reformed churches and Christian schools are swallowed up by the world.

The common grace *mentality* is hostile to antithesis, to spiritual separation, to the urgent biblical admonitions: "Be ye not unequally yoked...what fellowship...?...what communion...?...what concord...?...what part...?...what agreement...?...come out from among them, and be ye separate" (2 Cor. 6:14–18).

One may agree with the Protestant Reformed Churches or disagree, but can anyone say—in AD 2012—that the issue itself of common grace is insignificant, a mere distinctive?

The Unconditional Covenant

Another distinguishing doctrine of the Protestant Reformed Churches is the unconditional covenant, flowing out of and governed by the eternal decree of election. This is the doctrine that the covenant of grace, its gracious promise, its gracious blessings, and its gracious salvation have their origin in God's election, are governed by election, and are unconditional, as is election. That is, they depend upon the sovereign grace of God in Christ and not upon the sinner.

This doctrine applies Dordt and all the other Reformed confessions to grace and salvation in the covenant; views the covenant of grace as established with and carried out by Jesus Christ, the head of the covenant; gives assurance of salvation—*final* salvation—to every one in whom the grace of the covenant begins to work; and gives the glory of the beginning, the maintaining, and the perfecting of the covenant to God alone.

The alternative doctrine in Reformed churches is that of a gracious covenant with many more than only the elect. In this view, the covenant, its grace, its blessings, and its salvation are conditional, that is, depend for their continuance with a person, especially a baptized child, upon that person's deeds of faith and lifelong obedience.

However the proponents of the conditional covenant try to reconcile this doctrine with the truth of sovereign, particular grace in the Reformed confessions (and with the Bible, of which the confessions are the faithful expression), this doctrine teaches a covenant grace of God that is wider than election, that depends for its outcome in everlasting salvation upon the sinner, particularly the baptized child, and that is resistible. It also necessarily deprives Christ Jesus of the honor of headship of the covenant.

Who will say that ecclesiastical stands on these great, grand issues, concerning one of the most prominent, important truths in Scripture—the covenant of grace—are merely distinctives, nonessentials, regardless of which stand is taken? Surely, the truth of the gospel is at stake in these issues.

At the beginning of the twenty-first century, there has been significant development of the doctrine of a conditional covenant. Every Reformed and Presbyterian church in North America knows of this development. Many of the churches have been directly affected by the development. A number of the churches have had to deal with the development in their major assemblies.

I refer to the federal vision.

The federal vision is the development of the doctrine of a conditional covenant. The men of the vision themselves say so. The theology unmistakably shows this. The name expresses it.

The theology of the federal vision denies—*openly and in so many words*—justification by faith alone. Thus, it overthrows the sixteenth-century Reformation of the church. With its denial of justification by faith alone, the federal vision denies—*openly and in so many words*—the doctrines of grace confessed by the Reformed churches in the Canons of Dordt.

The federal vision teaches justification by faith and by the good works that faith performs. The federal vision teaches conditional election, conditional atonement, conditional (saving) grace in regeneration, and conditional preservation.

This development of the doctrine of a conditional covenant robs every believer of the assurance of everlasting life (he may yet fail to perform the conditions and fall away). Worse, it robs God of his glory regarding his greatest work (salvation depends, decisively, upon the works of the sinner).

If the Reformed churches are determined still to regard the controversy between the doctrine of an unconditional covenant and the doctrine of a conditional covenant as belonging to the category of nonessentials, they are mistaken. The mistake becomes increasingly inexcusable and increasingly difficult to make.

If the Protestant Reformed Churches begin now to view their knowledge and confession of the unconditional covenant as a mere distinctive, it will go hard with them both in time and in eternity in the judgment of God.

Marriage for Life

With regard to the Protestant Reformed doctrine and practice of marriage, they obviously concern the institution and relationship that is fundamental to earthly, human life. It is the basic relationship between humans—the male and the female. It is also basic to the family—the cornerstone of human society.

In addition, marriage is both the symbol of the covenant of grace between the real husband and the real bride, Jesus and his church, and a main means of God's gathering and rearing his church in the generations of married believers. Marriage is fundamental not only to human society, but also to the church.

Divorce and the remarriage that usually follows on the part of members of Reformed churches are not only the annihilation of the symbol of the covenant, but also the perversion of the symbol. The divorced and remarried couple in the church are a living testimony to the unfaithfulness of God in the covenant. Either he is represented as a husband who is unfaithful to his own wife, taking another woman, or he is represented as taking a woman who is not his wife, but the wife of another.

Divorce and the subsequent remarriage in the church are ruinous of the covenant children. The Bible says so, experience confirms it, and the children involved attest it—with anguish of heart.

Divorce and remarriage in the churches, today at nearly the same ungodly rate as in the unholy world, are a shameful witness to the watching world. Christian churches are as unfaithful to a fundamental calling of earthly life as is the world of the ungodly. Those who profess to be the children of light are as sensual as the children of darkness. The same breakdown of discipline and order characterizes the churches that characterizes the nations.

By the present day there are few, if any, Reformed churches in which divorce is permitted only for fornication and in which remarriage after divorce is strictly limited to the "innocent party." In most Reformed and Presbyterian churches, by their own admission if not by official church decision, there are remarried persons whose divorce was on the ground of something other than the sexual unfaithfulness of their mate, or who are married to persons divorced for some reason other than the fornication of their mate. Indeed, in many Reformed churches there are remarried men and women who were themselves the "guilty party."

Once the door of remarriage is opened, even a crack, it becomes impossible to stem the tide of divorce and remarriage for any and every reason—*within the churches.*

The same thing would happen in the Protestant Reformed Churches if they were to permit remarriage, at first, of course, only for the one whose mate has been guilty of sexual infidelity.

Human nature is the same everywhere and in everyone. It is not inclined to be faithful to one woman or to one man for life. In the difficulties that attend every marriage, it is prone rather to the easy divorce than to the hard work of reconciliation. It is lustful, desiring others than one's own "vessel." It puts carnal satisfaction and a warm, human relationship above the satisfaction of God's approval and a warm relationship with him. It is unwilling to suffer loneliness for a few years in view of everlasting communion with God and the saints. And this depraved human nature is cunning and strong—cunning and strong as Beelzebub.

At the present time, the prevalence of divorce and remarriage *in the churches* is paving the way to the approval of sodomy not only in the nations of the "Christian" West, but also in Reformed churches.

When evangelical Christians oppose the powerful movement on behalf of homosexual "marriage" (no Christian should ever recognize sodomite couplings as marriage, regardless that a lawless, antichristian state legalizes the couplings) with appeal to the sanctity of marriage, the world responds with guffaws that churches full of divorced and remarried persons have not a leg to stand on in opposing sodomite "marriages."

Were the issue not so grave, the argument of socially conservative politicians in the United States against homosexual "marriage" would be amusing. They contend that by God's institution (or, if they are more politically correct, by long, human tradition), marriage is the union of one man and one woman. In fact, they do not mean this. What they mean is that marriage is the union of one man with one woman after another, or the union of one woman with one man after another, until the marrying man or woman finds the one he or she wants, or runs out of sexual energy. And let the children be damned.

This is the world, one will respond.

Indeed it is, but the appalling lawlessness regarding marriage and the solemn promise by which marriage is constituted ("til death us do part") in the churches contributes to the homosexual juggernaut in the world. It certainly puts no stout barrier in the way.

If Reformed ministers, elders, and concerned laymen suppose that the sodomite movement poses no threat to conservative evangelical and Reformed churches, they deceive themselves. Already, prominent, influential evangelical and Reformed theologians have contended publicly for the churches' approval of "homosexual marriage." One is Paul K. Jewett, then at Fuller Seminary in California.[10] Another is Lewis B. Smedes, then member in good standing and theologian in the Christian Reformed Church (prior to the formation of the United Reformed Churches). Both appealed to the churches' easy approval of unbiblical divorce and subsequent remarriage. Smedes observed that Jesus had much more to say against divorce and remarriage than against homosexuality.

The same pressure from church members in hard marital circumstances and the same thinking that sacrifices biblical injunctions to sexual satisfaction and personal relationships that cause the churches to tolerate unbiblical divorce and remarriage will also work to cause the churches to tolerate homosexual unions. Or, as Smedes expressed it, if churches and parents could ignore the biblical prohibition against divorce and remarriage because of the hardships of their own, dear children, they can do the same regarding the prohibition against homosexuality, when their own children are involved.[11]

The teaching, defense, and practice of lifelong marriage, *really* between one man and one woman, is not a distinctive.

Labor Union Membership

Regarding the stand of the Protestant Reformed Churches against the membership of Reformed Christians in the labor unions in North America, I indicate the stand and its importance by a series of rhetorical questions.

Is the Reformed Christian workingman to live in obedience to

10. See Paul K. Jewett, *Who We are: Our Dignity as Human: A Neo-Evangelical Theology* (Grand Rapids, MI: Eerdmans, 1996), 290–350. Jewett argues for the church's acceptance of practicing homosexuals on the ground of the church's acceptance of divorce and remarriage.

11. Lewis B. Smedes, "Like the Wideness of the Sea," *Perspectives: A Journal of Reformed Thought*, 14, no. 5 (May, 1999): 8–12.

the lordship of Jesus Christ in the sphere of labor? (So also is the Christian businessman, but this is not the subject now.)

Does Christ the Lord reveal in Scripture his will for the Christian employee?

Does the will of Christ the Lord in the New Testament require the Christian workingman to submit to the authority of the employer, even though the employer may be unjust?

Is this will of Christ in harmony with the fifth commandment of the law? Does the fifth commandment apply to the creation ordinance of labor, as well as to the family and to the state?

Do the labor unions, by virtue of their very constitution, commit themselves to rebellion against the employer in the strike? Do they practice rebellion? Is it a fact that in the course of carrying out their strikes the unions practice violence, mayhem, and murder?

Is a Christian corporately responsible for the principles and practices of organizations he willingly joins? The rebellions, the intimidation, the goon squads, the destruction of the property of others, the injuries of the neighbor, the murders?

In joining a union, does a Christian affiliate with a "brotherhood" of ungodly men and women, thereby advertising himself as a brother to all the other members of the union?

Does a Christian as an aspect of his membership pay dues that he knows are contributing, enormously, to the godless agenda of left-wing, liberal politicians, who are actively working to stamp out the last vestige of Christianity in the United States?

The Protestant Reformed Churches are convinced by Scripture that the answer to all these questions is yes.

And this explains both their stand regarding membership in the labor unions and their conviction that this stand is no mere distinctive.

Essentials

These doctrines and practices that distinguish the Protestant Reformed Churches, belonging as they do to the essentials of true churches of God, are necessarily aspects of the three marks of the true church, as listed in Article 29 of the Belgic Confession. They concern the purity of the preaching of the gospel, the right administration of the sacraments (which includes barring those who are living impenitently in disobedience to the law of God), the proper administration of discipline, and the holy life that preaching, sacraments, and discipline have as their goal.

We bring these doctrines and practices up in our doctrine of the church, as also in our striving for precious church unity.

We take these doctrines and practices into account when we decide which church to join and of which church to remain a member.

We think all believers should.

CHAPTER SEVEN

The Judgment of Harold Camping

S TRICTLY SPEAKING, Harold Camping does not belong in this book. This book responds to criticism of *Bound to Join*. Harold Camping has not criticized *Bound to Join*. There is no reason to think that he has ever read the book. Indeed, there is every reason to suppose that he has not. As is typical of every cult leader, Harold Camping is a layman who reads only the Bible and a concordance. Even the creeds of the Christian church are ignored, except for criticism of them. To the source materials of the cult, Mr. Camping has added one new element: the calculator.

Nevertheless, Harold Camping demands a place in a work defending the instituted church against determined critics of the church and, as now becomes evident, in the face of a definite movement opposing the church—a movement that illegitimately claims for its product the title "house church."

Harold Camping properly occupies the concluding place, for he is the divine warning of our day upon the house church movement, as also upon every teaching that rejects or disparages the church institute and living membership in it. Those who refuse to heed the warnings of God's word against despising the church, he smites with judgment—the judgment of Harold Camping.

It is not Camping's well-known, cultic predictions of the end of the world that are the concern of this chapter. Nor is our concern the fanciful, allegorical, mad exegesis of Scripture that produced the predictions. Our concern is Camping's abolition of the church institute.

Even the world knows Camping's proud, disobedient predictions of the date of the coming of Christ and of the end of the world, for God purposed to expose and abase him and his disciples before the world. So seriously does God take attacks on the body and bride of Christ. Twice, and then a third time, Camping predicted a date on which Christ would come. The source of these acts of disobedience to the word of the Lord in Matthew 24:36, and of overweening folly, was Camping's unlearned, untrained, idiosyncratic interpretation of the Bible, especially his fooling around with the numbers in Scripture.

Both of these evils—prediction of the date of Christ's coming and unleavened, allegorical exegesis of the Bible—with all their disastrous consequences not only for Camping, but also for his followers, are directly related to his rejection of the instituted church.

Abolition of the Church Institute

Harold Camping rejects the church institute. He rejects it in the most thorough manner possible. He teaches that God himself has put an end to the church institute. The reason for Camping's fixing on 1994 as the date of God's abolition of the church of Christ is of no interest to us here, except to note that 1994 was the date of Camping's first prophecy of the end of the world. Because "1994 was the official end of the church age,"[1] it was also the end of the preaching and hearing of the gospel, the administration and use of the sacraments, and the exercise of discipline by elders in the church institute. Christ no longer saves in and by the church institute, regardless

---

1. Harold Camping, *The End of the Church Age…and After* (Oakland, CA: Family Stations, Inc., 2002), 125.

that churches may still preach the truth. All churches, therefore, are called by God to disband. The churches that refuse to disband automatically become synagogues of Satan. The divine call to all believers (issued, of course, by God's messenger in these end times, Harold Camping) is to separate from the church. All those who remain in instituted churches have, by virtue of this fact, taken the mark of the beast and are damned.

Whereas the Christian church, from apostolic days, has always confessed that *outside* the church institute is no salvation, Camping teaches that *inside* the church institute is no salvation. Whereas the creeds of Reformed and Presbyterian churches teach that there is *salvation* in the church institute, Camping teaches that there is only *damnation* in the church institute.

Having abandoned the church, on peril of their soul's salvation, in compliance with the command of Harold Camping, believers must meet in small gatherings with family, friends, and any others who may share their faith in Harold Camping. They must form a house church, although Camping would not call the religious meetings in homes "churches." Camping prefers "fellowships." At these gatherings, especially on the Lord's day, the faithful are edified and saved by listening to Family Radio, that is, the exposition of Scripture by Harold Camping.

Outside the Church

Thousands of professing evangelical Christians, perhaps tens of thousands, perhaps even hundreds of thousands, worldwide (for Camping's network of radio stations extends throughout the world), have done this. Included are many who formerly called themselves Reformed or Presbyterian. They have left the instituted church. They hold the preaching of the gospel in contempt. They despise the sacraments. They disdain the authority of the office of elder. They have no use for the ministry of mercy of the diaconate. The communion of saints extends no wider than their own family and, perhaps, a few fellow-followers of Camping in the neighborhood.

For them all the offices have passed away with the church institute.

Presumably many, if not most, of these church despisers remain outside the church, even though the world did not end in 2011, any more than it did in 1994, and even though in this way God exposed Mr. Camping not only as a charlatan, but also as a false prophet. This is the way apostasy works. Few repent and return. Christ warned concerning this very thing in his great sermon on the last days: "Many false prophets shall rise, and shall deceive *many*" (Matt. 24:11, emphasis added). In the language of 1 John 2:19, men and women go out from the church institute and seldom return.

These deceived people have taken their children and grandchildren—their generations—with them out of the church and into perdition. Camping *emphasized* that they must get their children out of the church, threatening that remaining in the church would mean the damnation of the children.

> The terrible truth is that children born into that congregation [a congregation marked as a true church by "faithful preaching"] may be under the hearing of good preaching, but if the Holy Spirit is not in the midst of that congregation [as he is not since 1994, according to Camping], they will not become saved there. That family has a serious problem that can be remedied only by leaving the congregation.[2]

Under the Wrath of God

Those who have left the church institute under the instruction and at the command of Harold Camping, and remain out-

2. Ibid., 108.

side the church impenitently, are under the wrath of God and lost.

They despise the church institute—the church institute that has the marks of the true church—as synagogues and strongholds of Satan. But this is the institution established by Jesus Christ: "I will build my church" (Matt. 16:18). This is the body and bride of Jesus Christ, which he loves and for which he gave his life (1 Cor. 12:27, 2 Cor. 11:2, Eph. 5:25). This is the "house of God, which is the church of the living God, the pillar and ground of the truth" (1 Tim. 3:15).

They refuse to honor the office of the preaching of the gospel, which is the authoritative position and activity of the chief prophet himself, and stop up their ears to men called and sent of Jesus Christ and by whom he himself speaks savingly to his people (1 Tim. 3:1–7, Rom. 10:13–17). The ascended Christ gives "pastors and teachers; For the perfecting of the saints, for the work of the ministry, for the edifying of the body of Christ" (Eph. 4:11–12). And he gives them "till we all come in the unity of the faith…unto a perfect man" (Eph. 4:13). Whoever refuses to hear Christ's preachers refuses to hear him: "He that heareth you heareth me; and he that despiseth you despiseth me; and he that despiseth me despiseth him that sent me" (Luke 10:16).

In the impenitent followers of Camping, outside the church institute, are fulfilled the prophetic words of the apostle to Timothy, pastor of an instituted church: "The time will come when they will not endure sound doctrine; but after their own lusts shall they heap to themselves teachers, having itching ears; And they shall turn away their ears from the truth, and shall be turned unto fables" (2 Tim. 4:3–4).

The sacraments, these blind followers of their blind leader dismiss as merely "ceremonial laws," obsolete, done away with, in the same category as the ceremonial laws of the Old Testament. Camping *forbids* them to use the sacraments. But baptism and the Lord's supper are holy ordinances of Jesus Christ himself (Matt. 28:18–20, Matt. 26:26–29). Jesus indicated the importance of baptism when he told his disciples, "He that believeth *and is baptized* shall be saved" (Mark 16:16, emphasis added). Concerning the supper, the apostle of Christ said that in administering this sacrament the church shows the "Lord's death til he come" (1 Cor. 11:26).

To refuse to partake of the supper is willfully to disobey the Lord's command, "Take, eat…Drink ye all of it" (Matt. 26:26–27). To partake of the supper unworthily is to be guilty of the body and blood of Christ (1 Cor. 11:27). What must be the guilt of those who, as much as they able, annihilate the sacraments!

Those misled by Camping permit no body of elders to govern them. But the office of elder in every church is of apostolic authority: "Ordain elders in every city, as I had appointed thee" (Titus 1:5). The Holy Spirit charges elders to "feed the flock of God which is among you, taking the oversight thereof" (1 Pet. 5:1–2). To all believers and their children comes the command from the church's head, "Remember them which have the rule over you…Obey them that have the rule over you, and submit yourselves: for they watch for your souls, as they that must give account" (Heb. 13:7, 17).

Thousands, perhaps hundreds of thousands (for the destructive influence of Harold Camping is widespread), now live and die outside the church of Christ, in which alone is salvation; contemptuous of the preaching of the gospel, which is the living voice of Jesus Christ; despising the sacraments, which is damning; and rebelling against the eldership, which is the royal rule over his kingdom of King Jesus.

Deceived

This is their dreadful condition because of the false teaching of Harold Camping *that the church institute is unimportant, indeed abol-*

ished, and that membership in the church institute is unnecessary, indeed wicked.

Camping has taught multitudes, including Reformed men and women, that the church institute has been done away with by God. "1994 was the official end of the church age."[3] "[All] churches and congregations have become desolate. God's judgment is upon them, the Holy Spirit is no longer in their midst, and Satan is ruling there."[4] "God is commanding us not to even pray for the churches. There is no hope of any kind for the local churches. We are not even to pray for them."[5]

Camping has commanded all churches to disband forthwith. "If a congregation decides to be obedient to this command, they can re-organize their congregation, that is, they change from being a church congregation to a fellowship of believers. The elders will no longer be elders."[6]

Camping has convinced many that the Spirit of Christ no longer works salvation in the church institute. "Salvation is not possible in the churches today because the Holy Spirit has been taken out of them."[7] "There is no longer any possibility of anyone becoming saved within the churches."[8] "It is no longer possible for people to be saved within the churches, *regardless of how faithful a congregation may try to be to the Bible.*"[9]

On the contrary, Camping has asserted, within the instituted churches is only damnation, so that all who remain members are under Satan's rule, subject to God's wrath, and liable to hell's pun-

3. Ibid., 125.
4. Ibid., 147.
5. Ibid., 197.
6. Ibid., 259.
7. Ibid., 199.
8. Ibid., 238.
9. Ibid., 255; emphasis added.

ishment. "God commands the believers to leave the churches and congregations...God warns that if we remain, we are subject to her [Babylon's, in Revelation 18:4] plagues. The plagues that God is speaking about means to be cast into hell forevermore, to experience eternal damnation."[10] "If he [any member of an instituted congregation] persists in disobeying God's command to depart out of the local church, it may be evidence that he has the mark of the beast."[11]

Turning the truth of the church's confession that outside the church is no salvation on its head, Camping has convinced many that salvation is to be found only outside the church: "He [God] is saving a great multitude that no man can number, but this salvation is outside of the churches."[12]

The multitudes now perishing outside the instituted churches have taken to heart Camping's instruction that no longer is there within the churches the preaching of the gospel, by which Christ saves his people, but that the saving teaching of the word of God, indeed *all* saving teaching of the word, now is found outside the churches. "There is a famine of hearing the Word of God...in...the churches and congregations...However, outside the churches, the true Gospel is still going out, and it will continue to go into all the world until Christ returns."[13] Where is the true gospel to be found outside the churches? "An organization like Family Radio," the main teacher in which, of course, is Harold Camping.[14]

If those professing to be Christians are to sit in their house fellowships without a qualm of conscience, they must be assured that God has done away with the sacraments so that there is no longer a divine command to use them, baptizing their babies and partaking of the

10. Ibid., 222.
11. Ibid., 195.
12. Ibid., 209.
13. Ibid., 144.
14. Ibid., 149.

Lord's supper. Camping has assured them of this. "The New Testament commands concerned with the ceremonial laws [*sic*] of water baptism and the Lord's Supper which should be obeyed within the churches and congregations…can no longer be obeyed…God has effectively ended the possibility of the observance of the New Testament ceremonial laws of water baptism and the Lord's Supper."[15]

Camping was vehement in warning against recognizing the authority of the body of elders in the church institute. "The church no longer has any divine authority…No individuals…have spiritual rule over the congregation."[16] "Even if the pastor is an exemplary example of a humble, faithful servant of Christ…the believers should depart out…The church age…has ended."[17]

As the last quotation expresses, the practical conclusion of Camping's theology of the church, or better, theology of the abolition of the church, was a command, as from God, to all believers without exception to leave the instituted churches. Whereas the Reformed confessions confront all believers with the demand that they are bound to join the true church institute and never for any reason to separate from it, Camping called all believers to *abandon* the church institute and under no circumstances to remain members of it.

> God does have a specific commandment for all believers, and that commandment is that they must depart out of their churches…God has given no exceptions to this command. He has commanded each and every believer to leave the churches.[18]

> It is God's plan that *all* the true believers are to leave the churches and congregations. God emphasizes this by indi-

15. Ibid., 236.
16. Ibid., 259.
17. Ibid., 288.
18. Ibid., 209–10.

cating that the Holy Spirit has been taken out of the midst of the churches so that there is no longer any possibility of anyone becoming saved within the churches.[19]

Judgment upon Camping

God's judgment upon Harold Camping is not our chief interest here. God has judged him by public exposure as a charlatan, as well as a false prophet. God has put him to shame before the world. The man is a laughingstock, and deservedly. If he does not repent, which is far more than mumbling, "I made a mathematical miscalculation," infinitely worse judgment is impending.

For judgment falls on Harold Camping on account of his grievous sin of despising the blood-bought body and bride of Christ in her genuine manifestation in true, instituted churches; on account of leading multitudes into the wilderness outside the church, where are no bread and water of salvation in the word and sacraments; and on account of bringing the glorious truth of the second coming of Christ into disrepute.

This judgment is closely related to Camping's own sin of separating from the church institute. He himself practiced what he preached, if, in fact, it was not a case of preaching what he had himself first practiced. Outside the church institute, where were no oversight by elders and, therefore, no safeguard against falling into egregious error (to say nothing of a synod in case the elders failed); no authority to require him to repent of bizarre and heretical views; no protection of his audience against Camping's destructive teachings; and no operation of the Spirit of Christ keeping and leading him in the truth or bringing him back when he strayed, Harold Camping taught false doctrine, freely, widely, and for a long time and deceived many. No

19. Ibid., 238; emphasis is Camping's.

doubt, he deceived himself, that is, was himself deceived by the great deceiver.

Camping's deep, shameful fall was the judgment of him by Jesus Christ. Pastors and teachers who occupy the teaching office of Christ in the church, by ordination, can and all too often do use the office for their own glory and self-advancement. In all kinds of ways, Christ humbles such preachers.

One who sets himself up as a teacher of believers, indeed *the* teacher of believers, while rejecting the office of Christ in the church institute, *necessarily* exalts himself and challenges the authority and ability of Christ. It is now not Harold Camping serving Christ, honoring Christ, and deriving all his teaching ability from Christ, but Harold Camping as the rival of Christ—teaching on his own authority, exercising his own abilities, and honoring himself. Christ destroys his rivals. God has set his Messiah on his holy hill of Zion (Ps. 2:6), not Harold Camping or any self-appointed teacher of house churches or house fellowships.

Camping, the Judgment upon the House Church

By the judgment of Harold Camping in this chapter, however, is meant God's judgment upon the house church movement and all low views of the church institute *in the form of Harold Camping*. Harold Camping *is* the judgment of God. He is the judgment of God upon all thinking and practice that disparage, and even challenge, the teaching of the Belgic Confession concerning the necessity of membership in a true, instituted church:

> Since this holy congregation is an assemblage of those
> who are saved, and out of it there is no salvation, that
> no person of whatsoever state or condition he may be,
> ought to withdraw himself, to live in a separate state from

it; but that all men are in duty bound to join and unite themselves with it.[20]

The advocates of house churches reject the instituted church as thoroughly as does Harold Camping, even though they are careful not to express their rejection as God's ending of the church age and even though they do not arrive at their rejection by means of Camping's allegorical exegesis.

They too vigorously defend informal gatherings of family and friends on the Lord's day for worship and edification in the place of the ordered assembly of the instituted congregation.

They too plead the sufficiency of reading the Bible together and of listening to an unordained man explaining and applying the Bible, denying the necessity of the preaching of the gospel by a man who is called to the ministry and trained.

They too despise the sacraments, if not by outright repudiation of them as mere "ceremonial laws," then by living contentedly outside the institute in which the sacraments are administered and used. But as the house church movement gains momentum and boldness, its proponents openly spurn the sacraments.

> Some people ask: "What about Communion, if you don't 'go to church'? Didn't Jesus give the command, talking of the bread and the wine, 'Do this in remembrance of me'?"...The impression I get from the Bible is that, just as worship was 'in the course of life' in the early church, so was remembering the Lord's death with bread and wine. These were the staple food and drink of the first century Mediterranean world...I am by no means convinced that

20. Belgic Confession, Article 28, in Schaff, *Creeds of Christendom*, 3:418.

> Jesus was commanding a 'rite,' a religious performance…
> He [Jesus] was simply saying that when believers shared
> a loaf of bread…and when they shared wine together,
> they were to remember His broken body and poured out
> blood.[21]

They too are comfortable conducting their religious gatherings, listening to whatever instruction comes along, and living their Christian lives without the oversight of a body of elders.

They too find the church institute unnecessary. Indeed, as Kevin Reed's spirited defense of his house church makes abundantly plain, the advocates of the house church, or house fellowships, share to a great degree Camping's criticism of all the instituted churches as apostate. The difference between Camping's declaration of the end of the church age and Reed's pronouncement that all the churches in North America are apostate is minimal.

They too adopt a cavalier attitude toward the creeds of the church. Camping criticized the creeds openly. "Some of the erroneous conclusions were even written into and became a part of very prestigious Confessions."[22] Ironically, in view of the opposition of Reformed and Presbyterian defenders of the house church to Articles 27–29 of the Belgic Confession, Camping singled out the Belgic Confession as especially fallacious: "Many statements in the Belgic Confession are not nearly as Biblical as they should be."[23]

They too, therefore, not only defend the right of believers to sever their membership in the instituted church and to live in separation from it, but also call believers out of the instituted churches unto the salvation of the house church, as a sacred duty.

---

21. Stan Firth, *Custom and Command: Encouragement from the Scriptures for an Unusual New Breed of Christians—with Some Answers for Those Who Might Feel Critical of Them* (London: J. S. Firth, 1996), 25.

22. Camping, *The End of the Church Age*, 79.

23. Ibid., 285.

Like Harold Camping, those promoting the house church have recourse to the Reformation's important distinction between the invisible church of the elect and the visible institute. No one who likes to be thought a Christian dares to reject the church totally. They make use of the distinction by appealing to the universal, invisible church of the elect *against this church's manifestation of herself as a true institute.* We belong, they exclaim triumphantly, to the invisible church of the elect; the visible institute is unimportant or extinct. Membership in the invisible church of election excuses, indeed justifies, rejection of the visible church.

This was Camping's ploy.

> We must remember that while the corporate, visible, external church is under the judgment of God, the invisible, eternal church, of which every true believer is a part, cannot be harmed in any way. It continues until the end of the world and goes on into eternity...The gates of hell can never prevail against the invisible, eternal church.[24]

Squarely athwart the house church movement, as it begins to gain ground even among professing Reformed and Presbyterian believers, stands Harold Camping—God's dreadful judgment upon the manmade house church in all its works and ways.

The judgment that is Harold Camping consists of a man who usurped the position of teacher, not of the church, for he abolished Christ's church, but of thousands who called themselves believers. No church called and ordained him. No presbytery examined and laid hands on him (1 Tim. 4:14).[25] Therefore, God did not authorize

24. Ibid., 233.
25. When a minister is ordained into office in a Protestant Reformed church, "ministers who are present shall lay their hands on his head" (Form for Ordination [or Installation] of Ministers of God's Word, in *Confessions and Church Order,* 287).

and qualify him to be a teacher of his people.[26] Harold prophesied, but God did not send him (Jer. 14:14–15).

The judgment is a man who, nevertheless, claimed to be the supreme teacher of the believers. To him alone, he said, was given to know the very date of the second coming of Christ and of the end of the world. To him was made known a truth hidden in the Bible that God had not shown to the greatest exegetes and theologians in the church's history—Augustine, Luther, Calvin. To him God revealed what he had not even made known to Jesus Christ (see Mark 13:32).

The judgment is also a teacher of the people of God who was not trained for the ministry of the word, particularly in the all-important science of exegesis, or the interpretation of Scripture.

Therefore, the judgment is a man whose interpretation of the Bible not only regarding eschatology, but also regarding every passage he handled is among the most absurd in all the long, dismal history of allegory. One thing is worse than allegorical interpretation of Scripture. That is *unlearned* allegorical interpretation.

The result was false doctrine, culminating not in the prediction of the date of Christ's return, which is mostly ridiculous, but in the decree of the abolition of the church institute and the corollary of the necessity of all believers to leave the church, which is wholly deadly.

No insignificant aspect of the judgment of Harold Camping is a man who set himself up as the supreme teacher of the people of God without the authoritative oversight of himself by a body of elders. That was a huge step toward his own ruin, leaving aside for a moment the ruin of the multitudes who heeded his teaching.

26. The Form for Ordination [or Installation] of Ministers of God's Word used in the Protestant Reformed Churches asks of every man who is to be ordained or installed in the office of pastor and teacher, "First… whether thou feelest in thy heart that thou art lawfully called of God's church, and therefore of God Himself, to this holy ministry?" (*Confessions and Church Order*, 286). First, the lawful call of God's church—the church *institute*—and *therefore* of God himself!

No teacher of the people of God, though the holiest and soundest, can endure as a faithful pastor and teacher apart from the government *of himself* by the office of the ruling elder. He is too weak, and Satan is too cunning. And Jesus Christ is jealous of his prerogatives. He governs his church, including the pastors and teachers, by the office of elder. That man who exalts himself as the teaching authority of Christian house churches, or of Christian house fellowships (pale, manmade imitations of Christ's church), apart from the office of elder, Christ himself will bring to ruin.

The judgment that is Harold Camping consists also of the thousands of professing Christians worldwide who were deceived and destroyed by Camping. The judgment is the *consequences* of Harold Camping. Thousands honored his false claim to be the teacher sent from God at the end of the ages. Thousands gave themselves to his utterly mistaken, utterly foolish explanations of the Bible, and to his false doctrines. Thousands obeyed his commands. Thousands not only separated themselves from the instituted churches, but also consigned the church institute to the ash heap. Thousands gave their money to his execrable ministry. Thousands have been injured, if not ruined, financially. Thousands hoped for the second coming of Christ in 1994, and then in 2011, and then again at a later day and hour in 2011. Thousands bore false witness to this grand event in the glorifying of Jesus Christ. Thousands had their hope—*the main, the ultimate, hope of the believer*—dashed in 1994 and then all over again in 2011. Thousands carry the guilt of having brought shame on the name of Christ by their folly. Thousands remain outside the church institute.

God has judged the house church movement. God has judged all thinking and practice at the beginning of the twenty-first century that despises and rejects, or merely disparages, the church institute. The judgment has been public. God has advertised it in the secular media worldwide. The judgment has been devastating: exposure as a mountebank and a false prophet; shame and ridicule—shame and ridicule *that are deserved*; the spiritual and financial ruin of many; and the bringing of reproach upon the church of Christ, upon the church's hope, and upon Christ himself.

The judgment is Harold Camping and the multitudes destroyed by him outside the church institute.

Heed the Warning!

Harold Camping and his house fellowship movement, therefore, are God's warning to the defenders and practitioners of house churches. Those who will not heed God's word as faithfully declared by Articles 27–35 of the Belgic Confession, by Chapter 25 of the Westminster Confession of Faith, and by Chapters 17–29 of the Second Helvetic Confession will be taught, like a balky mule, by the rod of God's judgments.

Let the self-styled teachers and rulers of the house church take heed to the judgment of Harold Camping! Outside the office of pastor and teacher, you have neither authority nor competency to perfect the saints, to do the work of the ministry, to edify the body of Christ (Eph. 4:11–16). Christ does not speak through you. Christ regards you as his rival. Teaching apart from any oversight of the office of elder, you are not guided and protected by the government of Jesus Christ. You are on your own. Worse, having made yourself ruler of what you and your gathering regard as the substitute of the flock of Christ—the church institute—in defiance of the rule of Christ, you have Christ against you.

Beware, O leader of the house church, of the judgment of Harold Camping!

Let the men, women, and children who suppose that they are hearing the word of God and worshiping as a house church take heed to the judgment of Harold Camping! Lacking the offices of Christ, you are no church. Not only do you not hear the living voice of the chief prophet and teacher of the church, Jesus Christ, through the preaching of the gospel by an ordained minister, but also you are now exposed to every foolish interpretation of Scripture or outright heresy. Whoever comes along, presenting himself as a teacher sent from God, possessing some charisma, making a show of piety and spirituality, and having a gift of gab, becomes your teacher.

Rejecting the Christ-ordained rule of a body of elders does not mean that you are subject to *no* ruler, but that you are now vulnerable to *any* ruler. The leader of the house church, or house fellowship, is your ruler. Answerable to no one, his rule can easily become the tyrannical, destructive rule of the cult leader, of a Harold Camping. You are now at the mercy of a man.

The Harold Campings of the house church movement are, or inevitably become, sovereign lords over their followers. Camping tolerated neither opposition to nor reflection on his commands, specifically his command to all to leave the church institute in which they were members. "Beware!" he thundered, "God's commands [that is, Camping's just-issued decree to leave all church institutes] are not subject in any way to the rationality of our minds...We [that is, his audience] *are simply to obey*."[27]

Beware, O practitioners of the house church, of the judgment of Harold Camping!

Heed the warning!

Do whatever is necessary to join the church institute that displays the marks of a true church: the preaching of the pure doctrine of the gospel; the pure administration of the sacraments as instituted by Christ; and the exercise of church discipline by a body of ruling elders.[28]

"Out of it there is no salvation."[29]

27. Camping, *The End of the Church Age*, 235; emphasis is Camping's.
28. Belgic Confession, Articles 28–29, in Schaff, *Creeds of Christendom*, 3:418–19.
29. Ibid., 3:418.

9781936054138